SALMON

THE COOKBOOK

edited by

BILL JONES

whitecap

Edited by Lesley Cameron
Proofread by Joan Tetrault
Cover and interior design by Jacqui Thomas
Food photography by Andrei Fedorov
Cover photography by Jeff Morgan / Alamy
Salmon image by Alamy

Printed and bound in Canada by Friesens

LIBRARY AND ARCHIVES CANADA CATALOGUING IN PUBLICATION

Jones, W. A. (William Allen), 1959-
    Salmon : the cookbook / Bill Jones, editor.

Includes index.
ISBN 1-55285-645-3

    1. Cookery (Salmon) I. Title.

TX748.S24S24 2005   641.6'92   C2005-900564-5

The publisher acknowledges the financial support of the Government of Canada through the Book Publishing Industry Development Program for our publishing activities.

SALMON

THE COOKBOOK

INTRODUCTION

SALMON ARE AMAZING CREATURES. One of the most thrilling sights I've ever witnessed took place on a moonlit night on the north coast of B.C. Pink salmon were marshalling at the mouth of a river by the hundreds, their fins and tails stirring phosphorescent plankton, which shimmered like the northern lights. I imagine it must be just as breathtaking to see a school of mature chinook slicing through the ocean, glimmering with metallic-coloured scales.

To chefs, salmon have always been the home-run fish on the menu. Moreover, diners love salmon's rich flavour and the variety of preparation styles. This book's recipes reflect the love affair that chefs and cooks have with salmon. Using every technique in our culinary arsenal, we chefs have created recipes for poached, roasted, and grilled salmon as well as for cured and smoked, and even raw salmon.

Salmon have always been significant to the aboriginal peoples of the northern hemisphere. On the coasts and thousands of miles inland along major rivers, First Nations people have rejoiced at the salmon's annual return, which assumes deep cultural significance far beyond the filling of bellies. The basis of many ceremonies and feasts, salmon have sustained an entire people through the lean winter months.

Salmon were once bountiful in North Atlantic waters, spanning northward from Nova Scotia to Scotland. By contrast, much of the salmon available today is farmed, produced from the genetic stock of Atlantic salmon. Wild Atlantic salmon are now scarce, the result of habitat destruction and poor resource management. West Coast salmon, while threatened like their Atlantic cousins, are relatively abundant, with a range extending from the pristine fjords and rivers of the northwest coast of North America to the waters off Japan and the Russian region of Kamchatka.

For generations, salmon were mainly a canned fish used to make sandwiches. Today's shoppers are pleased to find fresh salmon in most grocery stores. Buy fresh salmon that are plump and firm with little odour. The flesh should have a healthy sheen. As salmon age, or are poorly handled, their flesh cracks and flakes — avoid this salmon.

I find that salmon freeze well, particularly the whole fish. Defrost the fish slowly, de-bone, and wrap the fillets in paper towel to remove excess moisture before cooking. To eliminate the potential for worm-infested flesh, most sushi-grade salmon are pre-frozen and thawed.

Today, wild salmon are considered one of our premium foods. Rich in nutrients and fats, they are excellent sources of omega-3 fatty acids. Research has pointed to omega-3 as a super-food, a great benefit to the heart and nervous system.

Most wild salmon come from the Pacific Northwest, from Washington State, British Columbia, and Alaska. The best fish are troll-caught using a line and hook and are processed immediately to ensure maximum quality. Fish caught in the ocean (or at the mouth of big rivers) are the highest in quality.

As salmon migrate upstream, they feed off their bodies' resources and slowly deteriorate from the harsh journey through the fresh-water systems. Salmon strive to return to the streams and gravel beds of their birth and are often tattered and spent as they finally spawn, dying shortly after. Nature wastes nothing: the salmon carcasses provide food for a host of wildlife, including bears and eagles, and vital nutrients for the river ecosystems. Some rivers are home to excellent genetic strains of salmon, one of the best known being the Copper River sockeye, deep orange in colour and high in fat. Other river systems, like the Fraser and Skeena, contain equally impressive stocks of sockeye but aren't as well known (or perhaps simply less well marketed).

In general, there are five types of wild Pacific salmon available in the marketplace:

CHINOOK — *Oncorhynchus tshawytscha*

At the top of the heap for many fishermen and chefs, chinook are large (up to 120 lbs./54 kg), with a deep blue-green, spotted back. Known as the spring or king salmon, chinook vary in colour. Some chinook (sometimes called the white king salmon) have an ivory-hued flesh wonderful for smoking, while others, heavily laden with fat, have a deep red colour. Chinook are the best all-round salmon for every cooking technique.

SOCKEYE — *Oncorhynchus nerka*

Prized for its firm red-orange flesh, sockeye are a smaller salmon, weighing up to 7 lbs. (3.15 kg) with a well-oiled and flavourful flesh. The skin of the sockeye is a blue-tinged silver, and their bodies are slim and streamlined. Sockeye are an excellent all-purpose fish, renowned as the best salmon for cold-smoking and gravlax.

COHO — *Oncorhynchus kisutch*

Highly sought by sport-fishermen and legendary for its ability to leap, coho grow up to 15 lbs. (6.75 kg) and sport a bright silver skin. A fine red in colour, their flesh is fully flavoured and suitable for all cooking methods.

CHUM — *Oncorhynchus keta*

Chum, also known as keta or dog salmon, are abundant. They look like sockeye salmon with a silvery side with black specks and faint grid-like bars. Their flesh pink to medium red, chum salmon reach up to 10 lbs. (4.5 kg). Milder in flavour than the prime salmon species, chum are excellent when hot-smoked or candied and make a good choice for pan-frying.

PINK — *Oncorhynchus gorbushca*

The smallest and most plentiful of the Pacific salmon species, pink salmon live an average of two years, weighing up to 5 lbs. (2.2 kg). When caught in the ocean, they're sometimes marketed as silverbright. With a delicate flavour and pale pink flesh, pink salmon are somewhat mild compared to other salmon but have a delicate and pleasing texture. Pink salmon are well suited to dry-heat cooking such as pan-frying and roasting.

MARINADES & CURING

Marinated salmon tastes just like smoked salmon, which is more expensive to buy. You can use fennel in place of dill. Serve with thin slices of rye bread or with crackers. Serves 8 to 12 as an hors d'oeuvre.

GRAVLAX WITH DILL

INGREDIENTS

¼ cup	chopped dill	50 mL
1	2-lb. (1-kg) fresh boneless salmon fillet, skin on	1
3 Tbsp.	kosher pickling salt	45 mL
¼ cup	sugar	50 mL
½ tsp.	freshly ground black pepper	2 mL
½ tsp.	ground allspice	2 mL
¼ cup	vinegar	50 mL

METHOD

Put half the chopped dill in the bottom of a baking pan. Place the salmon fillet, skin-side down, on top of the dill.

Mix together the salt, sugar, pepper, and allspice in a bowl. Pat the salmon with the spice mixture. Pour the vinegar over the salmon and sprinkle with the remaining dill.

Cover the baking dish with plastic wrap and chill in the refrigerator with a brick on top of the wrap for at least 24 hours. Spoon the brine juices over the salmon occasionally.

To serve, wipe the salmon clean and place on a wooden board, skin-side down. Slice very thinly at an angle.

For an interesting contrast of texture and temperature, serve this salmon with hot, boiled new potatoes.
Serves 8 to 10 as an appetizer.

HONEY PICKLED SALMON

INGREDIENTS

2 1/2 lb.	boneless salmon, skin removed, cut into 1-inch (2.5-cm) chunks	1 kg
2 tsp.	salt	10 mL
1	small onion, peeled and cut into 1-inch (2.5-cm) rings	1

Pickling Mixture

1 cup	cider vinegar	250 mL
1 cup	water	250 mL
1/2 cup	fragrant honey	125 mL
1	bay leaf crumbled	1
1/2 tsp.	yellow mustard seeds	2 mL
1/2 tsp.	black mustard seeds	2 mL
1 tsp.	whole cloves	5 mL
1 tsp.	whole black peppercorns	5 mL
1 tsp.	whole white peppercorns	5 mL
1 tsp.	coriander seeds	5 mL

METHOD

Toss the salmon cubes with the salt and let sit for 30 minutes. Rinse and pat dry. Place in a large bowl and cover with the onion rings.

Combine the pickling mixture ingredients in a non-corrodible saucepan. Bring to a boil, reduce the heat to low and simmer, partially covered, for 45 minutes. Pour the hot pickling mixture over the salmon. Insert a knife or chopstick into the salmon and jiggle it to release trapped air bubbles. Cool to room temperature and refrigerate for at least 24 hours before serving. Keeps for 1 week.

To serve, drain the salmon from the pickling liquid and serve as is or mix with 1 cup (250 mL) sour cream, 1 Tbsp. (15 mL) coarsely chopped dill, and 1 Tbsp. (15 mL) finely minced green onion.

This tastes and smells just like pastrami, but with a salmon flavour. Serve it as an appetizer, on top of scrambled eggs or as the obvious — a sandwich on light sour rye bread. Makes approximately 1 1/2 lb. (750 g).

SALMON PASTRAMI

INGREDIENTS

10	medium cloves garlic, peeled and sliced	10
1	stalk celery, chopped	1
1/3 cup	salt	75 mL
1/4 cup	sugar	50 mL
2 Tbsp.	black peppercorns	30 mL
1 Tbsp.	coriander seeds	15 mL
1 Tbsp.	yellow mustard seeds	15 mL
10	whole cloves	10
6	bay leaves	6
1	whole dried chili pepper	1
1/8 tsp.	cinnamon	.5 mL
2 tsp.	paprika	10 mL
2 Tbsp.	Worcestershire sauce	30 mL
2 tsp.	liquid smoke	10 mL
1	1 3/4 – 2 lb. (800 – 900 g) boneless salmon fillet, skin on	1

METHOD

Combine the garlic, celery, salt, and sugar in a food processor.

Coarsely grind the peppercorns, coriander seeds, mustard seeds, cloves, bay leaves, and chili pepper. Add to the salt mixture with the cinnamon, paprika, Worcestershire sauce, and liquid smoke. Process until the garlic is finely chopped and the whole mixture is evenly wet.

Prick the skin side of the salmon fillet about 40 times with a pin. Spread one-third of the mixture over the skin and the remaining mixture on the top of the fillet. Wrap securely with plastic wrap and place on a tray. Cover with another tray and weight down with canned goods or bottles of water. Refrigerate for 4 days.

Unwrap the salmon and scrape off the marinade. Wash under cold water and pat dry. To serve, slice the salmon extremely thinly on the diagonal, starting at the tail end.

Makes 2 cups (500 mL)

HOMESTYLE SALMON ROE
CURED WITH APPLE JUICE & SEA SALT

INGREDIENTS

2 cups	salmon roe	500 mL
1 cup	apple juice	250 mL
1/4 cup	sea salt	50 mL
1 sprig	rosemary	1 sprig

METHOD

To clean the roe, place the salmon roe on a clean work surface. Place the skin-side down and, with the back of a knife, gently scrape the roe away from the connective tissue. Remove as much tissue as possible, leaving individual eggs. (*Note:* any strands of tissue left behind will turn white and thicken when cured and can be removed later.)

Place the eggs in a strainer and rinse with cold water. Place in a glass bowl and add the apple juice, salt, and rosemary. Cover with plastic film and place in a refrigerator for 1 hour. Drain, remove the rosemary, and place in a storage container with a tight-fitting lid. Chill for at least 1 hour. This can be kept for up to 1 week.

Serve on crackers smeared with cream cheese or as a garnish to your favourite salmon dish.

Succulent and tender, brined salmon is a favourite in my home. Cook it on the grill or in a hot oven. Don't hold your breath looking for leftovers. For an awesome appetizer, serve small pieces of this fish on croutons. Serves 6.

BRINED ATLANTIC SALMON
WITH WINE GASTRIQUE

INGREDIENTS

1 1/2 cups	dry white wine	375 mL
1/4 cup	white sugar	50 mL
2 Tbsp.	kosher salt	30 mL
2 tsp.	coriander seed	10 mL
2 tsp.	fennel seed	10 mL
2 tsp.	mustard seed	10 mL
1 Tbsp.	black peppercorns	15 mL
3	bay or kaffir lime leaves	3
1 Tbsp.	finely sliced fresh ginger	15 mL
1	star anise	1
1	lemon or lime, zest of, for brine	1
6	5-oz. (150-g) Atlantic salmon fillets	6
2 Tbsp.	minced fresh thyme or lemon thyme	30 mL
1 tsp.	cracked fennel seed	5 mL
to taste	freshly cracked black pepper	to taste
1 tsp.	mustard seed	5 mL

METHOD

To make the brine, combine the wine with the sugar, salt, coriander seed, fennel seed, 2 tsp. (10 mL) mustard seed, peppercorns, bay or lime leaves, ginger, star anise, and lemon or lime zest. Boil the mixture long enough to dissolve the sugar and salt, then simmer 10 minutes. Let cool.

Immerse the salmon fillets in the brine in a shallow dish for 15 minutes. If the fish isn't completely covered, turn it once or twice. Remove the fish from the brine, pat it dry, and sprinkle the thyme, cracked fennel seed, pepper, 1 tsp. (5 mL) mustard seed, and lemon zest on the flesh side. Drizzle the honey and olive oil over the seasonings.

Preheat oven to 400°F (200°C). Place the fish on a shallow baking sheet. Roast until cooked through,

continues on next page

1	lemon, zest of, for salmon	1
2 Tbsp.	liquid honey	30 mL
1 Tbsp.	olive oil	15 mL

Wine Gastrique
Makes about 3 Tbsp. (45 mL)

3 – 4 Tbsp.	sugar	45 – 60 mL
1/2 cup	white wine	125 mL
2 – 3 Tbsp.	champagne vinegar	30 – 45 mL
1/2 tsp.	cracked black peppercorns	2 mL
to taste	salt and pepper	to taste

10 to 20 minutes, depending on the thickness of the fish. Place on a serving platter and drizzle with Wine Gastrique.

Wine Gastrique

In a shallow sauté pan over high heat, caramelize the sugar without stirring, about 3 to 5 minutes. Slowly add the wine and reduce by half its original volume. Add the vinegar and reduce by one-third. Season with salt and pepper to taste.

How can you make something better? Candy it! You can use the whole salmon fillet, but the salmon bellies contain the most oil and will give a richer dish. Serves 4.

CANDIED SALMON

INGREDIENTS

1 lb.	trimmed salmon bellies	500 g
1 cup	soy sauce	250 mL
1 cup	brown sugar	250 mL
1/2 cup	white sugar	125 mL
1 Tbsp.	sesame oil	15 mL
1/4 cup	plum wine	50 mL
2 tsp.	minced garlic	10 mL
2 tsp.	minced fresh ginger	10 mL
1/2 tsp.	salt	2 mL
2 tsp.	lemon pepper	10 mL
1/4 cup	maple syrup	50 mL

METHOD

Wash the salmon and pat it dry. Combine all the other ingredients and pour over the salmon. Stir to make sure it's well coated with the marinade. Refrigerate and marinate for 2 days, stirring every 12 hours.

Remove the salmon from the marinade. If you have a smoker, smoke it for 2 hours at 80°F to 100°F (27°C to 38°C). Slow cooking on your barbecue works just as well. Heat it to low and cook the salmon for 2 hours. Add a few wood chips for extra flavour. I find that greener wood creates more smoke and that's good. If the wood chips are dry, soak them in water for 10 minutes before putting them on. Remember that they burn up fast, so put a little on at a time to make the smoke last the whole cooking time. A third method is to bake the salmon in the oven at 275°F (140°C) for about 1 hour.

You'll need a plastic or stainless steel container long enough to hold salmon fillets. Marinated salmon can be eaten uncooked, like gravlax, or cut into fillets and grilled or pan-fried. Makes about 4 lb. (2 kg).

MARINATED SALMON

INGREDIENTS

2 cups	salt	500 mL
2 cups	sugar	500 mL
1 bunch	pickling dill (usually available in late summer) or regular dill, roughly chopped	1 bunch
1 bunch	fresh cilantro, roughly chopped	1 bunch
1 tsp.	black peppercorns, crushed	5 mL
1 Tbsp.	coriander seeds, crushed	15 mL
1	4-lb. (2-kg) whole salmon, trimmed and filleted	1
	olive oil	

METHOD

Combine the salt and sugar. Mix in the herbs and spices. Sprinkle about one-half of the mixture into container. Lay in one salmon fillet at a time, skin-side down, and cover completely with the remaining mixture. Cover the container with plastic wrap and refrigerate for 24 hours, or let rest in a cool place (such as a basement) for 12 to 16 hours.

Scrape the marinade off the fillets and put them back in the container. Pour in enough olive oil to partially cover.

Cover the container and store in the refrigerator. This keeps for up to 10 days.

Serves 6 as an appetizer, 2 to 3 as a main course

SALMON MARINATED
IN LAPSANG SOUCHONG TEA

INGREDIENTS

1 tsp.	salt	5 mL
2 tsp.	sugar	10 mL
1	1-lb. (500-g) boneless salmon fillet, skin removed	1
1/4 cup	Lapsang Souchong tea	50 mL
1 Tbsp.	vegetable oil	15 mL

METHOD

Mix the salt and sugar together and sprinkle both sides of the fillet. Sprinkle both sides of the fillet with the tea, pressing it gently onto the fish. Cover and refrigerate overnight.

Scrape the tea from the salmon. In a heavy, non-stick skillet, heat the vegetable oil over medium-low heat. Place the salmon fillet in the skillet and cook until the outside is brown and crispy, about 3 to 4 minutes on each side. Remove from the heat and let sit for 1 minute before serving.

Miso is a fermented soy bean paste that's an excellent aid to digestion. Serves 4.

SEARED SPRING SALMON

CURED WITH MISO, GARLIC & CHILIES

INGREDIENTS

2 Tbsp.	light miso paste	30 mL
2	garlic cloves, minced	2
1	jalapeño pepper, seeded and minced	1
1 Tbsp.	light (or sushi-style) soy sauce	15 mL
1 Tbsp.	vegetable oil	15 mL
1 Tbsp.	honey	15 mL
1	1 1/2-lb. (750-g) spring salmon fillet, skin and pinbones removed	1
1 Tbsp.	olive oil	15 mL
1 Tbsp.	butter	15 mL
to taste	salt and pepper	to taste
1	lemon, juice of	1

METHOD

In a small bowl, combine the miso paste, garlic, jalapeño, soy sauce, vegetable oil, and honey.

On a flat work surface, cut the salmon into 1-inch (2.5-cm) thick slices. Place in a glass casserole dish and pour over the marinade. Cover with plastic wrap and chill for at least 1 hour.

In a non-stick skillet over medium-high heat, add the olive oil and butter. When sizzling, add the salmon in batches, season with salt and pepper, and cook until the salmon begins to char, about 1 to 2 minutes per side. Transfer to a serving plate and drizzle with the lemon juice. Serve warm or at room temperature.

This marinade can be used with any fish, but it's especially delicious with salmon. Grill vegetables along with the fish for a quick side dish. Serves 4.

BBQ SALMON

IN SOY SAUCE MARINADE

INGREDIENTS

1	1-lb. (500-g) salmon fillet, skin on	1
1/4 cup	soy sauce	50 mL
1/3 cup	rice vinegar	75 mL
1/4 cup	water	50 mL
1 Tbsp.	olive oil	15 mL
1 1/2 Tbsp.	honey	22 mL
1/4 cup	finely diced onion	50 mL

METHOD

Place the salmon skin-side up in a glass baking pan. In a small bowl, combine the soy sauce, vinegar, water, oil, honey, and onion. Pour the marinade over the fish and marinate in the refrigerator for 1/2 to 1 hour. Baste the fish frequently.

Grill the fish for 10 minutes per inch (2.5 cm), flipping it over halfway through cooking.

TIMESAVER TIP

Brush the salmon fillet with teriyaki sauce and grated ginger before cooking. Grill as above.

STOCKS, SOUPS & CHOWDERS

Salmon stock is strong fish stock. Just as the fish of the Mediterranean flavours the classic bouillabaisse, salmon gives our West Coast stocks a unique flavour. If you're using fish heads, be sure to remove the gills. Any fish can be substituted. Makes 8 cups (2 L).

SALMON STOCK

INGREDIENTS

1 lb.	salmon bones, washed (see next page)	500 g
1 Tbsp.	vegetable oil	15 mL
8 cups	cold water	2 L
1 cup	diced onion	250 mL
1/4 cup	diced carrot	50 mL
1/4 cup	diced celery	50 mL
1	leek, chopped	1
1	bay leaf	1
1 Tbsp.	chopped fresh basil	15 mL
1 Tbsp.	chopped fresh thyme	15 mL
1/4 cup	chopped green onion	50 mL
1 Tbsp.	salt	15 mL
1 Tbsp.	cracked black pepper	15 mL
1/4 cup	white wine	50 mL

METHOD

Toss the bones in the oil. Grill for 10 to 15 minutes over medium-high heat or roast in the oven for 1 hour at 325°F (160°C).

Put the bones in a pot large enough to hold the stock. Add the water and all the other ingredients. Bring to a simmer and cook for 1 hour. (Since the bones are small, a long period of cooking isn't needed.) Strain the stock through a fine mesh strainer or cheesecloth and chill over ice. Refrigerate for up to 4 days or freeze for later use.

MAKING STOCK

When making stock, always wash the bones first to get rid of the blood, which can cloud the stock and change its flavour. You can either wash the bones under cold water until the blood is gone or cook them in boiling water for about 1 minute, then drain and rinse. Roasting darkens the bones and cooks out the gelatin, which creates a richer stock. We grill the bones over alder to add a smoky flavour.

Serves 4

SALMON HOUSE
SEAFOOD CHOWDER

INGREDIENTS

6 cups	Salmon Stock (page 22)	1.5 L
1/4 cup	butter	50 mL
1/2 cup	diced onions	125 mL
1/4 cup	diced celery	50 mL
1/4 cup	diced carrots, peeled	50 mL
1/4 cup	all-purpose flour	50 mL
2 Tbsp.	tomato paste	30 mL
1/2 cup	canned plum tomatoes	125 mL
1/2 cup	tomato juice	125 mL
3/4 cup	Clamato juice	175 mL
1 Tbsp.	chopped fresh dill	15 mL
1 Tbsp.	chopped fresh basil	15 mL
1 Tbsp.	chopped fresh thyme	15 mL
3 Tbsp.	diced green onion	45 mL
1 tsp.	Worcestershire sauce	5 mL
1 tsp.	soy sauce	5 mL
1 tsp.	salt	5 mL

METHOD

Bring the stock to a simmer in a saucepan.

Melt the butter in a large stockpot over medium heat. Add the onion, celery, and carrot and sauté for 10 minutes. Add the flour, mix well, and cook for another 5 minutes. Add the tomato paste and cook for another 5 minutes. Stir in the hot fish stock until the mixture is smooth, stirring constantly to prevent lumping.

Add the tomatoes, tomato juice, Clamato, dill, basil, thyme, green onion, Worcestershire and soy sauces, salt, pepper, sugar, hot pepper sauce, zucchini, and red pepper. Bring to a simmer and cook for 30 minutes.

Add the shrimp, salmon, and mixed fish and simmer for another 10 minutes.

continues on next page

1 tsp.	black pepper	5 mL
1 Tbsp.	sugar	15 mL
1/2 tsp.	hot pepper sauce	2 mL
2 Tbsp.	zucchini, roasted and chopped	30 mL
2 Tbsp.	sweet red pepper, roasted and chopped	30 mL
5 oz.	shrimp	150 g
8 oz.	salmon, cubed	250 g
8 oz.	mixed fish, such as snapper, cod, halibut, etc., cubed	250 g

Celebrate spring with this fabulously fresh chowder. The combination of salmon, spring vegetables, and Dijon creates an unusual and inspired soup. Serves 4 to 6.

SALMON & SPRING VEGETABLE
CHOWDER WITH DIJON

INGREDIENTS

1 Tbsp.	unsalted butter	15 mL
1	onion, chopped	1
2	celery stalks, sliced	2
3 cups	low-sodium chicken or vegetable stock	750 mL
6 to 8	small red new potatoes, scrubbed and quartered	6 to 8
1 cup	baby carrots, scrubbed and halved	250 mL
12	asparagus spears, trimmed and cut diagonally in thirds	12
1 cup	low-fat milk	250 mL
2 Tbsp.	cornstarch	25 mL

continues on next page

METHOD

In a large saucepan, melt butter over medium heat. Add onion and celery; sauté for 4 minutes. Add stock, potatoes, carrots, and asparagus; bring to a boil. Reduce heat, cover, and simmer for 15 minutes.

Combine milk and cornstarch in a jar with a tight fitting lid, shake until well blended, and stir into the saucepan. Add salmon, mustard, lemon zest, and dill; simmer for 5 minutes until the soup starts to thicken slightly, stirring occasionally. Season with salt and pepper and serve garnished with fresh dill or parsley.

1	1-lb. (500-g) salmon fillet, skin removed, cut in bite-sized chunks	1
1 Tbsp.	Dijon mustard	15 mL
1 tsp.	lemon zest	5 mL
1 Tbsp.	finely chopped fresh dill or 1 tsp. (5 mL) dried dill	15 mL
to taste	sea salt and freshly ground pepper	to taste
for garnish	chopped fresh dill or parsley	for garnish

Rich and elegant with its green and pink colours, this soup makes a lovely first course. Although you could use spinach instead, it's the tart lemony flavour of the sorrel that sets this chowder apart. Serves 6 to 8.

SALMON SORREL CHOWDER

INGREDIENTS

6 cups	Salmon Stock (page 22)	1.5 L
1	3-lb. (1.5-kg) salmon fillet	1
1 Tbsp.	good-quality olive oil	15 mL
1/2 cup	finely chopped shallots	125 mL
8 oz.	fresh sorrel, washed and chopped	250 g
1/4 cup	butter	50 mL
1/2 cup	all-purpose flour	125 mL
1/2 cup	dry white wine	125 mL
1 cup	whipping cream	250 mL
to taste	salt and white pepper	to taste
for garnish	fresh chervil	for garnish

METHOD

Heat the olive oil in a large soup kettle on medium-high heat and sauté the shallots until soft. Add the sorrel and sauté until the sorrel has cooked down, about 7 to 10 minutes. Add the butter. When melted, stir in the flour. Cook, stirring, for 5 minutes or so, until the roux is well incorporated and foamy. Pour the wine in while whisking to prevent lumps. Add enough of the fish stock to thin to a heavy cream consistency and continue to simmer to concentrate the flavours and reduce slightly, about 15 minutes. Add the cream. Season to taste with salt and pepper.

Break the salmon fillet into pieces and add to the soup. Cook for another 10 minutes to heat thoroughly.

Garnish with fresh chervil.

This main-course soup is really a vegetable and corn chowder with a taste of salmon. Team it up with warm rolls and baby greens tossed with honey lemon dressing for a quick dinner. Serves 6.

SALMON & VEGETABLE SOUP

INGREDIENTS

2 tsp.	olive oil	10 mL
1/2 cup	chopped celery	125 mL
1/2 cup	chopped onion	125 mL
1/4 cup	chopped green bell pepper	50 mL
1	clove garlic, minced	1
3 cups	diced potato	750 mL
1 cup	sliced carrots	250 mL
1 cup	chicken broth	250 mL
1 cup	water	250 mL
1 cup	thinly sliced zucchini	250 mL
1	7 1/2-oz. (213-g) can pink salmon	1
1	13 1/2-oz. (385-mL) can evaporated skim milk	1
1	14-oz. (398-mL) can cream-style corn	1
1/4 cup	chopped fresh parsley	50 mL
1 tsp.	chopped fresh dill	5 mL
1/4 tsp.	ground black pepper	1 mL

METHOD

Heat the oil in a large saucepan over medium heat. Add the celery, onion, green pepper, and garlic. Sauté until softened, but not browned. Add the potato, carrot, chicken broth, and water. Bring to a boil. Simmer for 15 minutes, or until the potatoes and carrots are cooked. Add the zucchini and cook for 5 more minutes.

Break apart the salmon and crush the bones. Add the salmon and liquid, evaporated milk, corn, parsley, dill, and pepper to the vegetables in the pot. Heat through slowly, stirring often, until the soup is bubbly and hot.

NOTE

Cream-style corn isn't fatty as the name implies: it's simply creamy in texture and flavour. The bonus is that corn is a vegetable especially high in phytosterols.

Serves 6

CHILLED SALMON
TARTARE SOUP

<table>
<tr><td colspan="3">INGREDIENTS</td></tr>
<tr><td>1</td><td>Spanish onion, peeled and sliced</td><td>1</td></tr>
<tr><td>1</td><td>leek, cleaned and sliced</td><td>1</td></tr>
<tr><td>1</td><td>fennel bulb, trimmed and sliced</td><td>1</td></tr>
<tr><td>1</td><td>celery root, peeled and sliced</td><td>1</td></tr>
<tr><td>1</td><td>potato, peeled and sliced</td><td>1</td></tr>
<tr><td>10 cups</td><td>chicken stock</td><td>2.5 L</td></tr>
<tr><td>1</td><td>bay leaf</td><td>1</td></tr>
<tr><td>12</td><td>whole peppercorns</td><td>12</td></tr>
<tr><td>1</td><td>sprig of fresh tarragon</td><td>1</td></tr>
<tr><td>to taste</td><td>salt</td><td>to taste</td></tr>
<tr><td>2</td><td>cooked potatoes, diced</td><td>2</td></tr>
<tr><td>8 oz.</td><td>fresh salmon, very finely diced</td><td>250 g</td></tr>
<tr><td>1 tsp.</td><td>finely chopped dill</td><td>5 mL</td></tr>
<tr><td>1 tsp.</td><td>peeled and diced shallot</td><td>5 mL</td></tr>
<tr><td>1 tsp.</td><td>finely chopped capers</td><td>5 mL</td></tr>
<tr><td>to taste</td><td>salt and freshly ground black pepper</td><td>to taste</td></tr>
<tr><td>1 cup</td><td>plain yogurt</td><td>250 mL</td></tr>
</table>

METHOD

Put a large soup pot on the stove and add the Spanish onion, leek, fennel, celery root, sliced potato, stock, bay leaf, and salt to taste. Bring to the boil and simmer for 1 hour.

Purée the soup in a food processor and pass through a fine sieve. Refrigerate overnight. The soup will keep for two days.

On the day you wish to serve the soup, prepare the cooked potatoes and reserve at room temperature. Combine the salmon, dill, and shallot for the tartare. Season well with salt and pepper.

To serve, chill 6 soup bowls. Spoon some potato dice into each bowl. Mix together the soup, tartare, and yogurt. Taste and adjust seasoning. If the soup is too thick, adjust consistency with water.

Serve cold.

Serves 4

SALMON STEW

INGREDIENTS

5 Tbsp.	unsalted butter	75 mL
2	leeks, white and light green part only, thinly sliced	2
1 cup	zucchini, cut into 1/4 -inch (5-mm) dice	250 mL
1/4 cup	finely diced celery	50 mL
1/4 cup	finely diced carrots	50 mL
8 oz.	cultivated mushrooms, thinly sliced	250 g
3 Tbsp.	all-purpose flour	45 mL
2 cups	canned or bottled clam nectar	500 mL
1 1/2 lb.	boneless salmon fillets, skin removed, cut into 1/2 -inch (1-cm) cubes	680 g
1/2 cup	whipping cream, half-and-half cream or milk	125 mL
to taste	salt and pepper	to taste
2	green onions, thinly sliced	2
1 Tbsp.	finely chopped fresh parsley	15 mL
2 Tbsp.	finely chopped fresh dill	30 mL

METHOD

In a large saucepan, melt 3 Tbsp. (45 mL) of the butter over medium heat. Add the leeks, zucchini, celery, and carrots. Cook until the leeks are soft but not brown.

In a skillet, melt the remaining 2 Tbsp. (30 mL) butter over high heat; add the mushrooms and sauté until the mushrooms are tender and any liquid they have thrown off has evaporated. Reserve.

Add the flour to the leeks and stir for 1 minute. Turn the heat to high and slowly whisk in the clam nectar. Bring to a boil, turn down the heat and simmer for 10 minutes, stirring occasionally. Add the salmon and mushrooms. Simmer until the salmon is cooked through, about 10 minutes, stirring occasionally. Add the cream or milk and season with salt and pepper. When the stew is piping hot, add the green onions, parsley, and dill.

Serve in heated bowls.

This is the Horizons version of the classic French bouillabaisse. Serves 4.

HORIZONS SEAFOOD BOUILLABAISSE

WITH PARMESAN PESTO BRUSCHETTA

INGREDIENTS

2 Tbsp.	extra virgin olive oil	30 mL
1/4 cup	finely diced onion	50 mL
1 tsp.	finely diced jalapeño pepper	5 mL
1 tsp.	minced fresh ginger	5 mL
1 tsp.	minced garlic	5 mL
1 Tbsp.	fresh lemon juice	15 mL
1/4 cup	dry white wine	50 mL
1	14-oz. (398-mL) can plum tomatoes, chopped	1
2 cups	diced tomatoes	500 mL
3 cups	Salmon Stock (page 22)	750 mL
1/4 tsp.	black mustard seeds	1 mL
1/8 tsp.	crushed dried chilies	.5 mL
1/4 tsp.	ground turmeric	1 mL
1/4 tsp.	ground cumin	1 mL
1/4 tsp.	saffron	1 mL

continues on next page

METHOD

Heat the olive oil in a large saucepan over medium heat. Sauté the onion, jalapeño pepper, ginger, and garlic for 2 minutes. Add the lemon juice and white wine and cook for about 2 to 3 more minutes, or until the liquid is almost all gone. Add the plum tomatoes, diced tomatoes, fish stock, black mustard seeds, dried chilies, turmeric, cumin, and saffron. Bring to a boil, reduce the heat, and simmer for 15 minutes.

Add the mussels, clams, and scallops. Cook for 2 to 3 minutes, until the shells begin to open. Add the salmon, halibut, prawns, salt, and pepper. Simmer gently for 4 to 5 minutes, until the fish is cooked. Ladle into large bowls and garnish with chopped cilantro. Serve with the bruschetta.

16	mussels	16
16	manila clams	16
12	small scallops in the shell	12
7 oz.	salmon, cut into 1-inch (2.5-cm) cubes	200 g
7 oz.	halibut, cut into 1-inch (2.5-cm) cubes	200 g
16	tiger prawns, peeled	16
to taste	sea salt and freshly ground black pepper	to taste
¼ cup	chopped fresh cilantro	50 mL

Parmesan Pesto Bruschetta

2 Tbsp.	finely chopped toasted pine nuts	30 mL
¼ cup	finely chopped fresh basil	50 mL
1 Tbsp.	minced garlic	15 mL
2 Tbsp.	extra virgin olive oil	30 mL
¼ cup	diced tomatoes	50 mL
pinch	sea salt and freshly ground black pepper	pinch
⅔ cup	grated Parmesan cheese	150 mL
8 slices	baguette cut 1 inch (2.5 cm) thick on an angle	8 slices

Parmesan Pesto Bruschetta

Preheat oven to 425°F (220°C).

If you're using a food processor, place the pine nuts, basil, garlic, olive oil, diced tomatoes, salt, pepper and 2 Tbsp. (30 mL) of the Parmesan into the bowl and pulse to a paste. (If you don't have a food processor, you can mince the ingredients with a knife and then mash everything to a paste in a small bowl.) Spread the paste on the 8 pieces of baguette and top with the remaining cheese. Place on a cookie sheet and bake for 6 to 8 minutes, until the bread is toasted and the cheese has melted. Serve hot with the bouillabaisse.

SAFFRON

This aromatic, bright orange, intensely flavoured spice is sold in small packages in thread form. The threads are the stigma of a small crocus and have to be hand-picked, which is why saffron is so expensive. Luckily, a little saffron will go a long way. Store it in an airtight container in a dark place for up to 6 months.

I use grape seed oil in this recipe because it's a neutral oil and doesn't add any flavour. You can substitute any oil, keeping in mind that oils do add flavour. Serves 4.

SALMON HOUSE HOT POT

INGREDIENTS

1/4 cup	grape seed oil	50 mL
1	onion, cut into 1-inch (2.5-cm) triangles	1
1	carrot, peeled and thinly sliced on the diagonal	1
1	rib celery, thinly sliced on the diagonal	1
8 oz.	chorizo, cooked and sliced into 8 pieces	250 g
12	clams	12
12	mussels, washed and beards removed	12
8	tiger prawns, deveined	8
4	2-oz. (50-g) boneless salmon fillets, skin removed	4

continues on next page

METHOD

Heat the oil in a saucepan over medium heat and add the onion, carrot, celery, and chorizo. Cook for 5 minutes and add the clams, mussels, and prawns. Cook for about 2 minutes and add everything except the salt and pepper. Cover and simmer for 5 minutes. Season with salt and pepper. Divide the seafood evenly among 4 bowls and pour the broth over it.

12	snow peas	12
1	head bok choy, cut into quarters	1
1	finely diced small jalapeño pepper, stem and seeds removed	1
1/4 cup	chopped green onion	50 mL
2 Tbsp.	chopped cilantro	30 mL
1/4 cup	ginger wine	50 mL
4 cups	Salmon Stock (page 22)	1 L
to taste	salt and black pepper	to taste

Use your favourite fish and seafood. Similar to a classic bouillabaisse, this meal is served with a highly seasoned mayonnaise on the side. Serves 6.

SEAFOOD HOT POT

WITH SAFFRON AÏOLI

INGREDIENTS

2 Tbsp.	vegetable oil	30 mL
1	small onion, julienned	1
1	rib celery, diced	1
1	carrot, diced	1
2	cloves garlic, minced	2
1 cup	white wine	250 mL
3 cups	Salmon Stock (page 22)	750 mL
1 lb.	fresh mussels, debearded	500 g
4 oz.	fresh salmon, diced	125 g
4 oz.	fresh halibut, diced	125 g
4 oz.	tiger shrimp, deveined	125 g
4 oz.	bay scallops	125 g
1 tsp.	chopped fresh thyme	5 mL
1	tomato, diced	1
1	potato, cooked, peeled and diced	1
1/2 cup	corn or peas	125 mL

METHOD

In a large saucepan, heat the oil and sauté the onion, celery, and carrot until tender, about 5 minutes. Add the garlic and sauté 1 minute more. Add the wine and stock and bring to a simmer. Add the mussels, cover the saucepan, and simmer for 2 minutes. Then add the fish, cover, and simmer for 2 minutes more. Finally, add the shrimp, scallops, thyme, tomato, potato, and corn or peas and simmer, covered, for another 2 to 3 minutes or until the mussels open. Season with basil, dill, salt, and pepper immediately before serving.

To serve, ladle the hot pot into wide-mouthed soup bowls and spoon a dollop of saffron aïoli directly on top or onto a piece of toasted French bread on the side, to dip into the broth. Use whatever fish and shellfish are available. Delicate items need less cooking time and should be added near the end.

continues on next page

2 Tbsp.	shredded fresh basil	30 mL
1 Tbsp.	chopped fresh dill	15 mL
to taste	salt and pepper	to taste

Saffron Aïoli

3/4 cup	mayonnaise	175 mL
2	cloves garlic, minced	2
pinch	saffron	pinch
1	lemon, juice of	1

Saffron Aïoli

Stir together the mayonnaise and garlic. Combine the saffron and lemon juice and let them sit for a few minutes to allow the flavour and colour to be drawn out. Stir the juice into the mayonnaise.

CANAPÉS & SNACKS

Assemble this simplified sushi just before serving so that the base doesn't become soggy. Makes 80 canapés.

SUSHI STACK CANAPÉS

INGREDIENTS

1 cup	#1 grade sushi or short-grain rice	250 mL
1¼ cups	water	300 mL
2 Tbsp.	rice vinegar	30 mL
1 Tbsp.	granulated sugar	15 mL
1 tsp.	salt	5 mL
5	sheets nori (dried edible seaweed)	5

Toppings

4 oz.	thinly sliced smoked salmon or very fresh raw salmon or tuna	125 g
¼ cup	flying fish roe	50 mL
¼ cup	pickled ginger	50 mL
1 Tbsp.	wasabi paste	15 mL
2 Tbsp.	soy sauce	25 mL

VEGETARIAN VARIATIONS

Substitute shredded carrot and sliced avocado — or shredded green mango and sliced green onion — for the fish.

METHOD

Place the rice in a large, heavy saucepan and add the water, vinegar, sugar, and salt. Cover and place over medium-high heat until the water comes to a boil. Reduce the heat to low and boil (without peeking under the lid) for 15 minutes. Remove from the heat and let stand for 10 minutes. Remove the lid and transfer the rice to a cookie sheet.

Spread the rice out and let cool to room temperature. Do not refrigerate. (The rice can be made up to 4 hours ahead then covered with a clean, damp towel and stored at room temperature until needed.)

Cut each sheet of nori into 16 squares, using kitchen scissors. Place a spoonful of rice on top of each square. Top with thinly sliced fish and fish roe or your own topping choices. Serve immediately with pickled ginger, wasabi paste, and soy sauce for dipping on the side.

Kappa-maki is the Japanese name for a cucumber sushi roll. I have added smoked salmon in this elegant version.
For a quick dipping sauce, mix Japanese soy sauce with a small amount of wasabi. Makes 32 pieces.

SMOKED SALMON SUSHI ROLL

INGREDIENTS

4 sheets	pre-toasted nori	4
2 cups	cooked sushi rice (page 40)	500 mL
2 Tbsp.	powdered wasabi, mixed with 2 tsp. (10 mL) cold water	30 mL
4 oz.	smoked salmon, cut into strips	125 g
1	English cucumber, seeded and cut into strips	1

WASABI

Wasabi, sometimes referred to as Japanese horseradish, is the root of the wasabi plant. It comes in a powdered form or as a paste. Mix the powder with cold water or a little rice vinegar. The longer you mix the wasabi the stronger it becomes. It's available in Asian grocery stores or some supermarkets.

METHOD

Place one nori sheet, shiny side down, on a bamboo sushi mat. Distribute 1/2 cup (125 mL) of the rice over the nori sheet, leaving a 1/2 -inch (1-cm) margin at the top.

Dampen your hands with cold water and press the rice onto the nori. Spread a thin layer of wasabi along the centre of the rice. Cover the wasabi with one-quarter of the smoked salmon and cucumber. Lift the edge of the mat with your thumbs. Hold the ingredients in place with your fingers and roll the mat and nori to enclose the filling. Roll to the far edge of the rice. Moisten the edge of the nori with water and complete the roll. Press gently for a few seconds and unroll the mat. Repeat with the remaining sheets of nori.

Cut each roll into 3/4 -inch (2-cm) slices, wiping the knife between cuts. Serve with soy sauce. The sushi rolls can be made 8 hours in advance. Wrap them in plastic wrap and refrigerate until serving time.

I use the strong bursts of flavour from finely chopped shallots, capers, chilies, and lime juice to complement the rich silky texture of the smoked salmon. I always tell people to serve this on the new olive oil potato chips now available. They're quite thick, so they hold up well to the salmon mixture. Serves 4 to 6.

SMOKED SALMON TARTARE

INGREDIENTS

6 oz.	smoked salmon, diced	175 g
2 Tbsp.	capers, rinsed and chopped	30 mL
1	tomato, seeded and diced	1
1	shallot, diced	1
1/2 tsp.	sea salt	2 mL
1/2 tsp.	freshly ground mixed peppercorns	2 mL
1/2	lime, juice of	1/2

METHOD

Combine all the ingredients and toss gently. Check the seasonings, adding more salt and pepper if necessary. Let it sit for about 30 minutes before serving and check again for seasonings. You may have to add a little more lime juice.

Use either lox or hot-smoked salmon for this smoky dip. Serve with thinly sliced baguette or crackers.
Makes 1½ cups (375 mL).

SMOKED SALMON DIP

INGREDIENTS

1 cup	low-fat ricotta cheese	250 mL
2 oz.	smoked salmon	50 g
3 Tbsp.	chopped fresh dill	45 mL
2 Tbsp.	capers, rinsed	30 mL
1 Tbsp.	fresh lemon juice	15 mL
1 Tbsp.	horseradish	15 mL

METHOD

Process the ricotta until smooth in the food processor. Add the salmon, dill, capers, lemon juice, and horseradish. Process until blended.

TIMESAVER TIP

Buy smoked salmon-flavoured low-fat cream cheese. Add your own herbs and blend thoroughly for a fresh homemade touch.

Perfect party food for the fiddly-minded. For the less fiddly, scoop the mousse into several pretty bowls and smooth the tops. Top it with roe and simply arrange the mini blini on a plate around the bowl. Makes about 60 mini blini cornets.

MINI BLINI CORNETS

STUFFED WITH COLD-SMOKED SALMON MOUSSE & CRYSTALLIZED LEMON

INGREDIENTS

1 lb.	cold-smoked salmon	500 g
1 lb.	plain cream cheese (firm, not spreadable)	500 g
1 Tbsp.	minced lemon zest	15 mL
1 Tbsp.	fresh lemon juice	15 mL
1 – 2 Tbsp.	whipping cream	15 – 30 mL
2 Tbsp.	minced fresh chives	30 mL
1 Tbsp.	minced fresh thyme	15 mL
pinch	hot chili flakes or cayenne pepper	pinch
½ cup	salmon or flying fish roe, for garnish	125 mL
for garnish	fresh dill sprigs (optional)	for garnish

continues on next page

METHOD

Finely purée the salmon in a food processor. Add the cream cheese and blend well, scraping the bowl down once or twice as needed. Add the lemon zest and juice, whipping cream, chives, thyme, and chili flakes or cayenne. Pulse 2 or 3 times to blend, or stir in by hand. Chill until needed, but be sure to let the cold mousse stand at room temperature for at least 30 minutes before use so it's piping consistency.

To assemble, fill a piping bag fitted with an open star tip. Lay a row of mini blini in front of you on a flat tray and pipe a smooth curl or round of mousse onto the centre of each, making it large at one edge and tapering off to a tail at the other edge. Pinch 2 sides of the crêpe up at an angle so that the narrow end is completely closed and the fat end is completely open. It should look like a mini cornet. Decorate each mini blini with a tiny dollop of roe, a piece of crystallized lemon, and a sprig of fresh dill. Cover and chill until serving time.

Mini Blini

Makes several hundred 2-inch (5-cm) crêpes (or 24 6-inch/15-cm crêpes)

3/4 cup	all-purpose flour	175 mL
4	eggs	4
1 cup	milk	250 mL
1 Tbsp.	poppy seeds	15 mL
	salt	
1/4 cup	melted unsalted butter	50 mL

Crystallized Lemon

Makes about 1/2 cup (125 mL)

1/2 cup	lemon zest, coloured part only, thinly sliced	125 mL
1 cup	sugar	250 mL
for rolling	berry sugar	for rolling

A CRÊPE ON EVERY PLATE

Crêpe batter will happily wait for you in the refrigerator for up to 1 week. Even better, crêpes of any size will await your pleasure for 4 or 5 days, well wrapped, in the refrigerator, and almost indefinitely in the freezer. Suddenly, entertaining unexpectedly is easy. Think of wonderfully quick late-night apple crêpes with friends and simple brunch dishes for extra guests on Sunday mornings. A stack of these mini discs will transform into cute little cornets when you pipe a curl of smoked salmon mousse into their centre and fold the edges up.

Mini Blini

Mix together the flour and eggs, whisking well. Slowly add the milk and whisk to eliminate any lumps. Strain the batter though a fine mesh sieve and let it rest for at least 30 minutes. Stir in the poppy seeds, salt, and melted butter.

To make mini blini, heat a flat (not ridged) grill over medium heat. Lightly oil it if it requires oiling. Use a gravy ladle to spoon out a teaspoon (5 mL) of batter into a small circle about 2 inches (5 cm) in diameter. Fill the grill with blini. Flip them as they brown and cook briefly on the second side. Transfer the blini to a parchment-lined tray. Stack them tidily. Cool, then wrap and chill or freeze until needed.

Crystallized Lemon

Use these tender bites of flavour as garnish on desserts, especially chocolate and fruit, on ice cream, with pork dishes, and as garnish for smoked salmon dishes. A little goes a long way, so be sparing…what you don't use today will keep indefinitely in its syrup!

Put the zest into a small pot, cover with cold water, and bring to a boil. Drain. Replace the water and repeat the process twice more. The third time, add the sugar and bring to a boil. Simmer the zest in the syrup until it's tender, adding more water as needed. Pour the zest and syrup into a small glass jar, cover, and store at room temperature. For sugar-coated zest, dry the strands on a rack, then roll them in berry sugar.

Clever cooks learn many variations for the same ingredients. This salmon pâté has a different flavour because the salmon is smoked and cream cheese is substituted for butter. Serves 4 to 6.

SMOKED SALMON PÂTÉ
WITH DILL

INGREDIENTS

6 oz.	smoked salmon	175 g
8 oz.	cream cheese	250 g
2 Tbsp.	finely chopped shallots	30 mL
3 Tbsp.	fresh lemon juice	45 mL
3 Tbsp.	chopped dill	45 mL
to taste	freshly ground black pepper	to taste
for garnish	finely chopped dill	for garnish

METHOD

Put all the ingredients except the dill in a food processor. Process until smooth and chill in a small crock.

Before serving, garnish with finely chopped dill. This recipe can be thinned with the addition of a little mayonnaise and used as a dip with crackers or chips.

Potted fish is a traditional old English spread that uses boneless haddock, cod, or whitefish. I have used fresh salmon in this recipe, but you can also make it with canned sockeye salmon. If you use canned salmon, remove the bones, drain the salmon well, and omit the salt. Serve this spread with melba toast, Scandinavian flat bread, or poppyseed crackers. Makes 1 1/2 cups (375 mL).

POTTED SALMON

INGREDIENTS

2 Tbsp.	butter or margarine	30 mL
1	small onion, chopped	1
1	10-oz. (300-g) fresh salmon fillet, cut into 1-inch (2.5-cm) cubes	1
2 Tbsp.	dry white wine	30 mL
1 Tbsp.	fresh lemon juice	15 mL
1 tsp.	fresh thyme, or 1/8 tsp. (.5 mL) dried	5 mL
1	4-oz. (113-g) package cream cheese, softened	1
1/4 tsp.	salt	1 mL
1/8 tsp.	freshly ground black pepper	.5 mL

METHOD

Melt the butter in a large non-stick skillet over medium heat. Add the onion and cook about 5 minutes, until soft. Add the salmon cubes and white wine and cook for 3 minutes, or until the fish flakes with a fork. Cool slightly.

Combine the salmon, lemon juice, and thyme in a food processor or blender. Add the cream cheese and blend until smooth. Season with salt and pepper. Transfer to a serving bowl. Cover and refrigerate until serving time.

The spread can be made 2 days in advance, stored in a covered container in the refrigerator, and brought back to room temperature before serving.

An easy appetizer that can be made in minutes. If goat cheese isn't your favourite, use cream cheese for a simple alternative. Roasted vegetables can be substituted for the salmon for a vegetarian version. I often use the coloured flour tortillas that are readily available in supermarkets.

SMOKED SALMON PINWHEEL

INGREDIENTS

2 Tbsp.	olive oil	30 mL
3	large shallots, thinly sliced	3
1 lb.	goat cheese	500 g
1 Tbsp.	horseradish	15 mL
10	8-inch (20-cm) flour tortillas	10
to taste	freshly cracked black pepper	to taste
1 lb.	sliced smoked salmon	500 g
1	bunch fresh dill	1

METHOD

Heat the olive oil in a small skillet. Add the shallots and fry until crispy. Drain on paper towel. Combine the goat cheese with the horseradish and shallots.

Lay the tortillas flat on your work surface and spread the cheese mixture evenly over them. Generously grind pepper over the cheese. Place the smoked salmon on top of the cheese in a single, even layer. Place some dill in the centre of each tortilla, forming a line down the centre.

Firmly roll the tortilla up, jelly-roll fashion. Make sure it's tight so it won't come apart when slicing. Wrap each roll tightly in plastic wrap and chill until serving time.

To serve, slice on the diagonal into $1/2$-inch (1-cm) slices.

I borrowed this dish from Hugh Carpenter and tweaked it a bit. I was thrilled to reduce the number of chicken satés out there while still providing an easy and tasty appetizer. Makes 18 satés.

SESAME-CRUSTED SALMON SATÉS
WITH ORANGE GINGER

INGREDIENTS

18	6-inch (15-cm) bamboo skewers	18
1	12-oz. (375-g) salmon fillet, skin removed	1
1/4 cup	oyster sauce	50 mL
2 Tbsp.	orange juice concentrate	30 mL
1 Tbsp.	soy sauce	15 mL
1	clove garlic, minced	1
1 Tbsp.	grated fresh ginger	15 mL
3 Tbsp.	chili paste	45 mL
1/4 cup	honey	50 mL
1 Tbsp.	sesame oil	15 mL
2 – 3 Tbsp.	toasted sesame seeds	30 – 45 mL

METHOD

Presoak in water 18 bamboo skewers for at least 30 minutes. Slice the salmon into thin strips. Weave the strips onto the presoaked skewers and set aside.

In a bowl, combine the oyster sauce, orange juice concentrate, soy sauce, garlic, ginger, chili paste, honey, and sesame oil, stirring thoroughly. (The marinade can be made ahead of time and kept in the refrigerator.) Brush half the marinade onto the salmon and let sit for 10 minutes. Heat the grill to medium. Grill the salmon for 1 to 2 minutes on each side. Brush the remaining marinade on the cooked salmon and sprinkle with the toasted sesame seeds.

These grilled Mexican sandwiches make a delicious appetizer when served with a bowl of fresh-tasting fruit salsa. Makes 16 pieces.

SMOKED SALMON QUESADILLAS
WITH SALSA

INGREDIENTS

1	4-oz. (113-g) package cream cheese, softened	1
1 tsp.	fresh lemon juice	5 mL
2 Tbsp.	lemon zest, finely chopped	30 mL
1 Tbsp.	chopped fresh dill	15 mL
4	8-inch (20-cm) flour tortillas	4
4 oz.	smoked salmon, thinly sliced	125 g
1/4 cup	finely diced red onion	50 mL
2 tsp.	vegetable oil	10 mL
1 cup	your favourite salsa	250 mL

METHOD

Combine the cream cheese, lemon juice, lemon zest and dill.

Arrange the tortillas on your work surface and spread the cream cheese mixture evenly over half of each tortilla. Place the smoked salmon on top of the cheese. Sprinkle with red onion. Fold each tortilla in half and gently press to seal.

Heat 1 tsp. (5 mL) of the oil to medium-high in a large, non-stick skillet. Place 2 tortillas in the pan and cook for 1 minute, until they're lightly browned. Turn them over and cook for another minute, until they're brown and the filling is warm. Repeat with the remaining oil and tortillas. Cut each quesadilla into 4 wedges. Serve immediately with the salsa.

Hot-smoked salmon is less expensive than cold-smoked salmon or lox, but it can be equally delicious. It's sold in small pieces at most seafood counters. Makes 24 pieces.

HOT-SMOKED SALMON
ON MINI NEW POTATOES

INGREDIENTS

12	mini red or white new potatoes	12
1/2 cup	sour cream	125 mL
2 tsp.	chopped fresh dill	10 mL
to taste	salt, pepper, fresh lemon juice, horseradish	to taste
12 oz.	hot-smoked salmon, skin removed, flaked into pieces	375 g
24	small dill sprigs	24

METHOD

Cut the potatoes in half. Trim a little from the uncut side so they will sit flat. Boil the potatoes in lightly salted water until just tender. Drain well and cool to room temperature.

Set on a serving tray cut-side up. In a small bowl combine the sour cream and chopped dill. Season to taste with salt, pepper, lemon juice, and horseradish.

Spoon a small amount of this mixture on top of each potato. Top with a piece or two of flaked salmon. Garnish with a dill sprig and serve.

ERIC'S OPTIONS

For a richer version of this dish, top the salmon with a small spoon of caviar before garnishing with dill. Other seafood — such as crabmeat, thinly sliced lobster meat, or salad shrimp — can replace the smoked salmon.

With a little artistic licence, the delicious duo of salmon and corn becomes an easy and elegant starter. Keep it simple or dress up the presentation by stacking a stylish layered tower of blini and salmon, topped with a cloud of wasabi cream and long thin chives. Don't worry about having extra wasabi powder — it's great in mashed potatoes or mixed with soy sauce and maple syrup and drizzled over salmon. Makes 6 to 8 servings.

CORN BLINI

WITH SMOKED SALMON & WASABI CREAM

INGREDIENTS

1 cup	sweet corn kernels (use canned or tiny frozen corn)	250 mL
4	large eggs	4
1/3 cup	all-purpose flour	75 mL
1 1/2 cups	whipping cream	375 mL
1/2 tsp.	salt	2 mL
to taste	freshly ground white pepper	to taste
2 Tbsp.	finely minced chives and dill	30 mL
1 tsp.	wasabi powder	5 mL
2 Tbsp.	finely minced chives, dill, chervil, tarragon or a combination	30 mL
1/4 cup	melted butter	50 mL
12 – 16	slices smoked salmon, lox-sliced	12 – 16
for garnish	fresh herb sprigs	for garnish
2 tsp.	tobiko or red caviar for garnish (optional)	10 mL

METHOD

Purée the corn in the food processor or blender. Add the eggs, flour, 1/2 cup (125 mL) of the whipping cream, salt, pepper, and the 2 Tbsp. (30 mL) minced chives and dill. Blend well and set aside to rest for 20 minutes before using.

Blend a small amount of the remaining 1 cup (250 mL) whipping cream with the wasabi to wet the powder. Whisk the wasabi paste back into the whipping cream and continue to whip until firm peaks form. Fold in the 2 Tbsp. (30 mL) of minced herbs. Chill until ready to serve.

To cook the blini, melt enough butter to coat the skillet (a non-stick skillet may require less). Using a ladle, drop the corn batter in to create small cakes about 2 – 3 inches (5 – 8 cm) across. Turn the cakes when golden brown edges have formed and dry bubbles appear on top. Repeat in batches, adding more butter as needed. Hold the blini in a warm oven until you're ready to assemble and serve them.

To serve, arrange 3 – 4 warm blini in a circle with the edges overlapping. Top each piece with smoked salmon, shaping or rolling the salmon to fit on each blini. Add a dollop of the whipped wasabi herb cream to the centre of the plate. Garnish with herb sprigs. For a special touch, add a bit of caviar.

NOTE

Sour cream may be substituted for the whipping cream for a sauce that can be drizzled on or added as a dollop in the centre. Low-fat sour cream may be used since it's not cooked. Refrigerate after blending to allow the sour cream to thicken.

TOBIKO IS...

a bright orange, finely grained roe that makes a nice complement to salmon. It's available in Japanese markets and at most fish vendors that carry caviar or sushi supplies. Unused portions may be kept frozen for later use.

Dipping the salmon in the batter first and then in the flour gives a slightly different texture to the finished batter.
Serves 4.

SALMON IN BUTTERMILK ALE BATTER
WITH PACIFIC WAVE TARTAR SAUCE

INGREDIENTS

1 cup	all-purpose flour, for batter	250 mL
2 cups	buttermilk	500 mL
1 cup	Okanagan Spring Pale Ale or other pale ale	250 mL
pinch	cayenne pepper	pinch
1 tsp.	salt	5 mL
1/4 cup	minced onion	50 mL
12	2-oz. (50-g) boneless salmon fillets, skin removed	12
4 cups	vegetable oil	1 L
2 cups	all-purpose flour, for dredging	500 mL
8	lemon wedges	8

continues on next page

METHOD

Combine 1 cup (250 mL) flour, buttermilk, ale, cayenne, salt, and onion. Don't overmix. Soak the salmon in the batter for 2 hours.

Heat the oil to 350°F (175°C) in a deep, heavy pot. Dredge the salmon in the flour. Fry the salmon in batches so the fillets aren't overcrowded. Fry each batch for about 5 minutes. Drain on paper towels. Serve with lemon wedges and tartar sauce.

Pacific Wave Tartar Sauce

Makes 1 cup (250 mL)

2 Tbsp.	mayonnaise	30 mL
2 Tbsp.	sour cream	30 mL
2 Tbsp.	plain yogurt	30 mL
1 Tbsp.	capers, drained	15 mL
1 Tbsp.	minced onion	15 mL
1 tsp.	chopped fresh parsley	5 mL
1 tsp.	grated horseradish	5 mL
1 tsp.	washed, chopped Greek olives, pits removed	5 mL
1 tsp.	chopped stuffed green olives	5 mL
2 Tbsp.	hamburger or hot dog relish	30 mL
dash	Worcestershire sauce	dash
dash	hot pepper sauce	dash
1/2 cup	ketchup	125 mL
1 tsp.	fresh lemon juice	5 mL
pinch	salt and black pepper	pinch

Pacific Wave Tartar Sauce

Place everything in a bowl and mix well. Keep refrigerated. If the mayonnaise is fresh, the tartar sauce will keep in the refrigerator for 3 days.

A very popular lunch item, this has everything you look for in comfort food. Serves 4.

SALMON MELT

WITH TARTAR SAUCE & COLESLAW

INGREDIENTS		
4	4-oz. (125-g) boneless salmon fillets, skin removed	4
pinch	salt and black pepper	pinch
1/4 cup	vegetable oil	50 mL
1/2 cup	butter	125 mL
2 Tbsp.	chopped fresh dill	30 mL
1/4 tsp.	black pepper	1 mL
1/2	lemon, zest and juice of	1/2
4	slices baguette, 1 inch (2.5 cm) thick, sliced diagonally	4
8 oz.	Swiss cheese, in 12 thin slices	250 g
1/2 cup	thinly sliced red onion	125 mL
4	sprigs dill	4
4	wedges lemon	4
3/4 cup	Pacific Wave Tartar Sauce (page 55)	175 mL
4	large lettuce leaves	4

continues on next page

METHOD

The salmon fillets should be sliced thinly and about 4 inches (10 cm) long. Season with salt and pepper. Heat the oil in a skillet over medium-high heat. Sear the salmon on both sides, for about 1 minute per side. Remove from the skillet and keep warm.

Put the butter and dill in a food processor. Add the pepper, lemon juice, and zest. Combine until well mixed.

Butter the baguette slices with the dill butter. Place them butter-side down in the same skillet and fry until the butter browns. Remove the baguette slices and place them butter-side up on a baking sheet.

Divide the salmon among the baguette slices. Cover the salmon with the slices of Swiss cheese. Top with the red onion. Place under a broiler to melt the cheese and lightly cook the onion. Place each baguette slice on a plate and top with a sprig of dill. Serve with a lemon wedge and the tartar sauce on the side. Place the coleslaw in a leaf of lettuce to stop the dressing from running.

Coleslaw

Makes 4 servings

2 cups	shredded green cabbage	500 mL
1/4 cup	grated carrot	50 mL
2 Tbsp.	grated onion	30 mL
2 Tbsp.	apple cider	30 mL
1 tsp.	sugar	5 mL
1/4 tsp.	dried mustard	1 mL
1/4 tsp.	salt	1 mL
2 Tbsp.	minced fresh ginger	30 mL
1 Tbsp.	vegetable oil	15 mL

Coleslaw

Combine the cabbage, carrot, and onion in a bowl. Whisk together the cider, sugar, mustard, salt, and ginger. Pour over the cabbage mixture and toss. Add the oil and mix again.

The appeal of smoked salmon paired with potato is heightened by transforming the lowly potato into a delicate crêpe. Serves 6 to 8.

SMOKED SALMON
ON POTATO CRÊPES WITH CHIVE SOUR CREAM

INGREDIENTS		
1	large Yukon Gold potato, peeled	1
3/4 tsp.	salt	4 mL
1	whole egg	1
3 Tbsp.	all-purpose flour	45 mL
1/2 cup	2% milk	125 mL
2 Tbsp.	unsalted butter, melted	30 mL
1/2 cup	sour cream	125 mL
2 Tbsp.	finely chopped fresh chives	30 mL
6 – 8 oz.	smoked salmon	175 – 250 g

METHOD

Grate the potato very finely and sprinkle immediately with salt to prevent browning. Combine well with the egg, flour, milk, and melted butter. Heat a Teflon or crêpe pan over medium-high heat and grease lightly. Drop in spoonfuls of the crêpe mixture and spread thinly around the pan. Cook the crêpe until top surface is dry and then turn to brown the other side for 1 or 2 minutes. Crêpes can be made smaller (3 per person) or larger (1 per person) and stored in the refrigerator until ready to use. Simply heat in a low oven, 250°F (120°C).

Combine the sour cream with the chives. To serve, fold slices of smoked salmon over the potato crêpes and spoon sour cream over the salmon.

This is a very versatile recipe for cocktail parties, a dinner course, or even part of a champagne brunch. Top with caviar for an extra treat.

APPETIZERS

This is a light and colourful way of serving salmon. We serve it cold but it can also be served hot. We call it roulade because of the way it's rolled up, somewhat in the style of beef roulade. Serves 4.

SMOKED SALMON ROULADE

INGREDIENTS

1 lb.	spinach, washed and trimmed	500 g
1 cup	grated Parmesan cheese	250 mL
6	eggs, separated	6
1/2 tsp.	salt	2 mL
1/2 tsp.	black pepper	2 mL
3/4 cup	cream cheese	175 mL
1 tsp.	chopped fresh dill	5 mL
1 tsp.	chopped fresh basil	5 mL
1 Tbsp.	fresh lemon juice	15 mL
10 oz.	sliced smoked salmon	300 g

METHOD

Preheat oven to 350°F (180°C). Line a 12 x 15-inch (30 x 38-cm) cookie sheet with parchment paper.

Blanch the spinach in salted boiling water for 1 minute. Place under cold water to chill, then squeeze out as much water as possible. Chop the spinach and put it in a food processor. Add the cheese, egg yolks, salt, and pepper. Pulse until well mixed and transfer to a bowl.

Beat the egg whites to the stiff peak stage. Fold the spinach mixture into the egg whites. Spread the mixture evenly onto the prepared pan. Bake for 10 minutes. Remove from the oven and cool.

Place the cream cheese, dill, basil, and lemon juice in the food processor. Pulse until smooth and spreadable. Spread the herbed cream cheese over the spinach soufflé. Place the smoked salmon on the cream cheese. Roll it up like a jelly roll and cut it into slices. You can serve it right away or refrigerate it for up to 3 or 4 days.

Serve as an elegant first course or as part of a tapas-style dinner. Serves 4.

SALMON CARPACCIO

WITH MUSHROOM SALAD & SHAVED PARMESAN

INGREDIENTS

1	12-oz. (375-g) fresh, boneless salmon fillet	1
2 Tbsp.	fresh lemon juice	30 mL
1/2 tsp.	salt	2 mL
1	clove garlic, cut in half	1
1/2 cup	olive oil	125 mL
8 oz.	firm white mushrooms	250 g
1/4 cup	fresh basil leaves	50 mL
1 Tbsp.	coarsely chopped fresh parsley	15 mL
to taste	freshly ground black pepper	to taste
	large chunk of Parmesan or grana padano cheese	

METHOD

Slice the salmon into micro-thin slices and lay on a large platter close together but without overlapping. Cover with plastic wrap and refrigerate until needed.

Place the lemon juice, salt, and garlic in a small bowl and beat well with a fork. Slowly beat in the olive oil. Set aside.

Thinly slice the mushrooms. Tear the basil leaves into small pieces and add half to the mushrooms, along with the chopped parsley.

To serve, beat the dressing well to recombine and drizzle half of it over the salmon. Grind pepper to taste over the salmon.

Combine the remaining dressing with the mushrooms and mix well. Place the mushroom salad in the centre of the platter or plates of salmon. With a vegetable peeler, shave long shreds of cheese over the salmon and mushrooms. Scatter the remaining half of the basil leaves on top and serve immediately.

This appetizer can be made into individual portions using ring moulds, which can be cut from 4-inch-wide (10-cm) PVC pipe. For a single torte, a cake mould can be used. Whitefish caviar is light in texture, colour, and flavour. Although it's not uncommon, whitefish caviar might not be available. Flying fish roe is an appropriate substitute. Serves 6.

CUCUMBER RICOTTA TORTE
WITH SMOKED SALMON & PELEE ISLAND CAVIAR

INGREDIENTS

2	English cucumbers	2
dash	salt	dash
dash	sugar	dash
splash	rice wine vinegar	splash
1¹/2 lb.	ricotta cheese	750 g
2	shallots, minced	2
2 Tbsp.	fresh basil chiffonade	30 mL
2 tsp.	finely chopped fresh mint	10 mL
2 tsp.	finely chopped fresh chives	10 mL
1 tsp.	finely chopped fresh marjoram	5 mL
to taste	salt and pepper	to taste
6 oz.	smoked salmon	175 g
1	2-oz. (57-g) jar Pelee Island whitefish caviar	1
for garnish	balsamic vinegar and olive oil	for garnish

METHOD

Thinly slice the cucumbers into rounds and toss gently with the salt, sugar, and vinegar. This adds flavour and softens the cucumbers for easier shaping. Let sit 10 to 20 minutes.

Meanwhile, mix the ricotta with the minced shallots and herbs and season to taste. To assemble the tortes, place ring moulds onto a plastic wrap-lined baking sheet. Line the bottom of the moulds with cucumber slices, overlapping slices. Using the same overlapping technique, line the inside rims of the moulds. Spoon equal amounts of ricotta filling into each mould. Place 1 or 2 slices of smoked salmon over the ricotta. Layer overlapping cucumber slices on top of the salmon.

The tortes can be prepared up to 6 hours in advance and chilled until ready to use. To serve, place each torte on individual plates using a spatula and gently slide the mould off. The moisture from the cucumbers prevents any sticking. Spoon a little caviar on top. Herb stems or finely diced peppers as a garnish add a beautiful colour to the surface of the plate. Drizzle a little balsamic vinegar and olive oil around the outside of the torte just before serving.

For a lunch entrée, serve the tortes on a bed of lightly dressed salad greens.

Serves 4

SMOKED SOCKEYE SALMON
& TOMATOES WITH CITRUS DRESSING

INGREDIENTS

1	lemon, juice and zest of	1
1	lime, juice and zest of	1
1 Tbsp.	orange marmalade	15 mL
1/4 cup	mayonnaise	50 mL
1 Tbsp.	water	15 mL
to taste	salt and black pepper	to taste
1/4 lb.	smoked sockeye salmon, thinly sliced	125 g
1 lb.	tomatoes	500 g
to taste	salt and black pepper	to taste
1	green onion, thinly sliced	1

METHOD

Place the lemon juice and zest, lime juice and zest, orange marmalade, mayonnaise, and water in a mixing bowl. Whisk to mix and season with salt and pepper.

Arrange the salmon slices around the outside edge of a large platter. Cut the tomatoes into bite-size wedges (leave small tomatoes whole) and mound in the centre of the platter. Season with salt and pepper. Drizzle the citrus dressing over the tomatoes and garnish with the green onion. Serve immediately.

SALMON SORREL CHOWDER | page 28

Ellen Kelly — *Dishing*

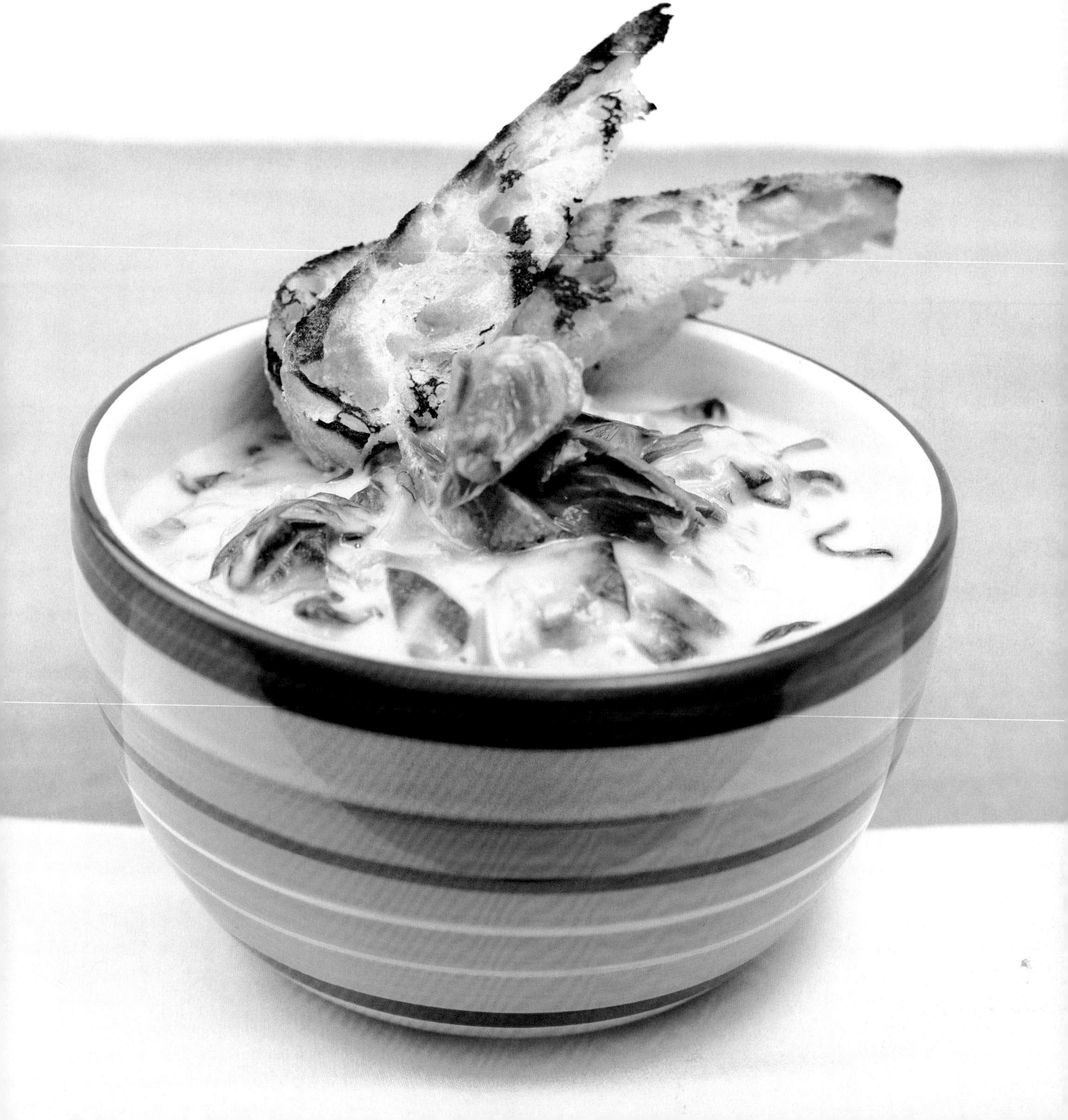

SEAFOOD HOT POT WITH SAFFRON AÏOLI | pages 36 – 37

Anna & Michael Olson — *Inn on the Twenty*

SMOKED SALMON TARTARE | page 42

Karen Miller — *Double Dishing*

SESAME-CRUSTED SALMON SATÉS WITH ORANGE GINGER | page 49

Judy Wood — *Double Dishing*

This recipe is ideal for summer gatherings. You can prepare the salmon and sauce in the morning when the kitchen is cool, refrigerate it, and have it ready to go when your guests arrive. *Serves 8.*

BAKED CHILLED SALMON FILLETS
WITH DILL & HORSERADISH SAUCE

INGREDIENTS

8	6-oz. (175-g) salmon fillets	8
1	lemon, juice of	1
2 Tbsp.	olive oil	30 mL
to taste	salt and freshly cracked black pepper	to taste
for garnish	cucumber slices, lemon wedges and dill sprigs	for garnish

Dill and Horseradish Sauce

3/4 cup	sour cream	175 mL
3/4 cup	mayonnaise	175 mL
2 Tbsp.	horseradish	30 mL
2 tsp.	chopped fresh dill	10 mL
2 tsp.	Dijon mustard	10 mL
to taste	salt, freshly cracked black pepper, and lemon juice	to taste

METHOD

Preheat oven to 425°F (220°C).

Place the salmon on a baking tray with sides. Drizzle with the lemon juice and oil. Season with salt and pepper. Cover and bake for 12 to 15 minutes. Remove from the oven, uncover, and cool to room temperature.

Carefully transfer the salmon to a serving platter. Wrap and refrigerate until well chilled. Decorate the salmon with cucumber, lemon wedges, and dill. Place the sour cream, mayonnaise, horseradish, fresh dill, and mustard in a bowl and mix well to combine. Serve the sauce alongside the salmon.

ERIC'S OPTIONS

Use other fresh herbs — such as tarragon, chives, and mint or a combination of them — instead of the dill in this recipe. If you prefer a spicier sauce, increase the amount of horseradish and Dijon mustard.

Crab cakes are an hors d'oeuvre staple from coast to coast, but what could be more fitting on the West Coast than a salmon cake? Indian candy-style salmon makes a cake like no other. Makes 36 patties.

INDIAN CANDY CAKES

WITH LEMON DILL AÏOLI

INGREDIENTS

1 lb.	Indian candy	500 g
1/3 cup	finely chopped green onion	75 mL
1/2 cup	finely diced green pepper	125 mL
1 Tbsp.	grainy Dijon mustard	15 mL
1/4 cup	finely chopped fresh parsley	50 mL
2 Tbsp.	prepared horseradish	30 mL
1 tsp.	piri piri sauce, or any hot sauce	5 mL
1	large egg, beaten	1
1/3 cup	good-quality whole-egg mayonnaise	75 mL
to taste	sea salt and freshly ground black pepper	to taste
3/4 cup	fresh white bread crumbs	175 mL

continues on next page

METHOD

Flake the salmon into a large mixing bowl, removing any visible bones. Add the onion, green pepper, mustard, parsley, horseradish, hot sauce, egg, and mayonnaise. Mix well to combine, and season with salt and pepper. Stir in the bread crumbs, adding more if the mixture is too moist. Form into small patties.

Sauté the cakes over medium heat in a non-stick skillet until they're golden brown, about 3 minutes on each side. Serve warm or at room temperature with the aïoli.

INGREDIENTS — continued

Lemon Dill Aïoli

Makes 1 cup (250 mL)

3	cloves garlic, peeled	3
2 Tbsp.	fresh lemon juice	30 mL
1/4 cup	fresh dill sprigs	50 mL
1	egg yolk	1
3/4 cup	extra virgin olive oil	175 mL
to taste	sea salt and freshly ground black pepper	to taste

METHOD — continued

Lemon Dill Aïoli

Purée the garlic, lemon juice, and dill in the bowl of a food processor. Add the egg yolk and pulse to mix. With the machine running, slowly pour the olive oil through the feed tube until a thick sauce forms. Adjust the seasoning with salt and pepper.

Serve with the salmon cakes. If you omit the dill, you can use it wherever aïoli is called for.

Hot-smoking gives a drier effect and a smokier taste for the salmon. It's not quite as dry as a jerk but it has a similar flavour. Serves 4.

HOT-SMOKED SALMON
WITH WARM HORSERADISH CREAM & SPICY CORNBREAD

INGREDIENTS

1/4 cup	butter	50 mL
1/2 cup	minced onion	125 mL
1/2 cup	fresh horseradish, peeled and grated	125 mL
2 cups	whipping cream	500 mL
1/2 tsp.	salt	2 mL
1/2 tsp.	black pepper	2 mL
1 tsp.	sugar	5 mL
1/2 tsp.	fresh lemon juice	2 mL
1 lb.	hot-smoked salmon, unsliced	500 g

Spicy Cornbread
Makes 1 loaf

1 cup	all-purpose flour	250 mL
2 Tbsp.	sugar	30 mL
1 Tbsp.	baking powder	15 mL
1 tsp.	salt	5 mL
1/2 tsp.	chili powder	2 mL

continues on next page

METHOD

Heat the butter in a medium saucepan until it bubbles. Add the onion and horseradish and sauté for 1 minute. Add the cream. Bring to a simmer and cook until reduced by half. Add the salt, pepper, sugar, and lemon juice.

Grill the smoked salmon for 10 minutes over medium heat. Cut into 4 pieces, top with a little sauce, and serve with the warm cornbread.

Spicy Cornbread

Preheat oven to 350°F (180°C). Line a 9 x 5-inch (2 L) loaf pan with silicon or parchment paper.

Sift the flour, sugar, baking powder, salt, chili powder, and black pepper into a bowl. Stir in the cornmeal and crushed chilies. Grate in the butter and mix well. Add the grated cheeses and mix well.

Purée the peppers and combine with the buttermilk and eggs. Fold the mixture into the dry ingredients.

pinch	black pepper	pinch
1 cup	cornmeal	250 mL
1 tsp.	crushed chilies	5 mL
2 Tbsp.	chilled butter	30 mL
1/4 cup	grated Parmesan cheese	50 mL
1/4 cup	grated Cheddar cheese	50 mL
1/4 cup	grated Swiss cheese	50 mL
1/4 cup	red bell pepper, stem and seeds removed	50 mL
1	jalapeño pepper, stem and seeds removed	1
1 cup	buttermilk	250 mL
2	eggs, lightly beaten	2

Don't overmix. Pour the batter into the prepared pan and smooth the top. The pan should be almost full. Bake in the centre of the oven for 1 hour, rotating the pan halfway through the baking time so it will cook evenly. Cool slightly in the pan, then remove the loaf and cool on a rack.

This terrine can be sliced thinly and placed on toast points. The Basil Mousseline is a light-tasting accompaniment that adds a summery flair to this delicate terrine. Prepare this a day ahead as the terrine needs time to set. Serves 12.

TERRINE OF SALMON, SCALLOPS
& MONKFISH WITH BASIL MOUSSELINE

INGREDIENTS

1 1/2 cups	whipping cream	375 mL
2 slices	white bread, crusts removed, torn into pieces	2 slices
1 lb.	fresh salmon, skin and pinbones removed	500 g
4 oz.	shrimp, peeled and deveined	125 g
2	eggs	2
3 Tbsp.	white wine	45 mL
to taste	salt and pepper	to taste
4 oz.	sea scallops, cut into quarters	125 g
4 oz.	monkfish, diced	125 g

continues on next page

METHOD

Combine half the cream with bread. Allow the bread to soak and set aside.

Place the salmon and shrimp in a food processor and blend for 30 seconds. Add the eggs and bread-cream mixture and blend until smooth. While blending, add the white wine, remaining cream, salt, and pepper.

To test for seasoning, bring a small saucepan of water to a simmer and drop a small spoonful of terrine base mixture into it. Poach until cooked. Cool and taste. Adjust seasoning if necessary. Remove the terrine base from processor and fold in the scallops and monkfish.

Preheat oven to 300°F (150°C).

Line a lightly oiled loaf pan or terrine mould with parchment paper, leaving some paper overhanging. Fill the mould with terrine mix until it reaches the top. Fold over any extra parchment paper and cover the top with foil. Place the mould in a roasting pan filled with 1 1/2 inches (4 cm) boiling water. Cook for 30 minutes,

Basil Mousseline

1/2 cup	whipping cream	125 mL
1 cup	mayonnaise	250 mL
2 Tbsp.	fresh basil chiffonade	30 mL

until the terrine registers an internal temperature of 150°F (65°C). Allow the terrine to cool and refrigerate for at least 12 hours before cutting. Serve with Basil Mousseline.

Basil Mousseline

Whip the cream to soft peaks. Fold in the mayonnaise and add basil. This can be prepared a few hours ahead of time, to allow the flavours to meld.

To make this recipe you'll need an enamelled cast iron terrine or pale form with a lid. The standard one is about 10 inches (25 cm) long and 3 inches (8 cm) wide. As with so many great dishes, the most intense work is in the preparation. Serving this recipe is as easy as slicing bread. Dishes like this are good for dinner parties because you can be with your guests and still serve an interesting dinner. Serves 6.

WARM TERRINE

OF SALMON & SCALLOPS

INGREDIENTS

3	leeks, split and washed	3
1	3-lb. (1.5-kg) salmon fillet	1
to taste	salt and freshly ground black pepper	to taste
1 lb.	sea scallops	500 g
1	clove garlic, finely chopped	1
1 Tbsp.	pastis or sambuca	15 mL

METHOD

Put a large soup pot of water on to boil. Blanch the leeks, leaf by leaf, in the water for 1 minute. Carefully line the terrine form with the blanched leeks, leaving an overhang of 2 inches (5 cm) on each side. Cut the salmon into pieces that fit the interior of the terrine. Cover the entire bottom of the terrine with 1 layer of salmon. Season liberally with salt and pepper.

Purée ¼ lb. (125 g) of the scallops in a food processor. Season with salt and pepper, garlic, and pastis. Fold the remaining whole scallops into the purée. This mixture is the next layer in the terrine.

Put a final layer of salmon fillet on top of the scallop mixture. Season liberally with salt and pepper. Fold the overhanging pieces of leek over the salmon. Put the lid on the terrine.

Preheat oven to 350°F (180°C).

Find a roasting pan that's longer than the terrine form. Line it with a clean tea towel and place the terrine form on the towel. Fill two-thirds of the roasting pan with hot water. Place the roasting pan with the terrine form in the oven. After 10 minutes, check the interior temperature of the terrine with a meat thermometer. The terrine is ready when the interior temperature reaches 150°F (65°C).

Invert the terrine onto a cutting board. You can serve it warm, straight out of the oven, or you can chill it and serve it cold with mayonnaise and a salad. If you decide to serve it warm, the best accompaniments are fresh steamed potatoes and vegetables. In either case, use a sharp carving knife to cut the terrine into 1/2-inch (1-cm) slices.

This version of a favourite childhood dish adds a touch of horseradish and anchovy to give it piquancy. These fish cakes can be served for brunch, lunch, or dinner. They can be made with cod or other fish in place of salmon, and you can vary the herb, using chervil or tarragon instead of chives. Sometimes I replace the flour with cornmeal. Serves 4.

SALMON & CHIVE FISH CAKES

INGREDIENTS

2 cups	cooked salmon, bones removed	500 mL
3 cups	mashed potatoes	750 mL
2	eggs, beaten	2
1/4 cup	chopped chives	50 mL
2 Tbsp.	finely chopped parsley	30 mL
1 tsp.	horseradish	5 mL
1 tsp.	anchovy paste	5 mL
to taste	freshly ground black pepper	to taste
	all-purpose flour	
1/4 cup	vegetable oil	50 mL

METHOD

Mix together all the ingredients, except the flour and oil, in a large bowl. Form the mixture into round cakes. Dust with flour.

Heat the oil in a skillet. Fry the cakes for 5 minutes per side until golden. Place on a serving platter in a warm oven until ready to serve.

EGGS & PASTRY

Salmon is a fish of international fame and the pride of the Pacific Northwest. About three-quarters of the large West Coast catch goes to the canneries, but when salted and smoked, salmon is a gourmet's delight. Serves 3 to 4.

SMOKED SALMON SCRAMBLE

INGREDIENTS

4 oz.	smoked salmon	125 g
	or	
1	3¹/2-oz. (100-g) can smoked salmon	1
6	eggs, lightly beaten	6
¹/4 cup	milk	50 mL
to taste	salt and pepper	to taste
1 Tbsp.	butter	15 mL
for garnish	chopped parsley	for garnish

METHOD

Break the salmon into small pieces and set aside.

In a bowl, crack the eggs, add the milk, and whisk to mix. Season with salt and pepper.

Heat a skillet over medium heat and add the butter. Pour in the eggs and top with the salmon. Stir with a spatula until cooked but still soft.

Garnish with chopped parsley.

Serves 4

FRITTATA WITH SMOKED SALMON,
ASPARAGUS & WHITE CHEDDAR

INGREDIENTS

1 Tbsp.	butter	15 mL
1	small onion, peeled and diced	1
1 cup	trimmed and chopped asparagus	250 mL
4	eggs	4
1 Tbsp.	water	15 mL
1 Tbsp.	chopped parsley	15 mL
to taste	salt and pepper	to taste
1/2 cup	smoked salmon, chopped	125 mL
1/4 cup	shredded white cheddar	50 mL

METHOD

Preheat the broiler to high.

In a large non-stick skillet over medium-high heat, add the butter and onions. Sauté until soft and beginning to brown. Add the asparagus and sauté for an additional 5 minutes or until the asparagus is soft and tender. Season with salt and pepper.

In a small bowl, break the eggs and whisk with the water. Add the parsley and season well with salt and pepper. Add the eggs to the asparagus mixture and stir with a spatula. Top the eggs with the smoked salmon and finally the cheese. Cook for 2 to 3 minutes or until the eggs begin to set. Place the skillet under broiler and cook until the cheese bubbles and begins to brown, a further 2 minutes. Remove from the oven and let sit for 1 minute. Serve warm.

This is a good recipe for a cheese appetizer. It can be served warm right from the oven or chilled from the refrigerator. The smoked sockeye salmon adds a rich, smooth, smoky flavour. Makes one 4 x 12-inch (10 x 30-cm) loaf pan.

SMOKED SOCKEYE
SALMON CHEESECAKE

INGREDIENTS		
1/2 cup	grated Parmesan cheese	125 mL
2 Tbsp.	butter	30 mL
1/2 cup	minced onion	125 mL
1/2 tsp.	minced garlic	2 mL
1 1/2 lb.	cream cheese	750 g
4	eggs	4
1/2 cup	whipping cream	125 mL
1/2 lb.	smoked salmon, puréed	250 g

METHOD

Preheat oven to 300°F (150°C).

Line a 4 x 12-inch (10 x 30-cm) pan with parchment paper. Brush with butter and sprinkle with a little of the Parmesan cheese.

Melt the butter in a sauté pan over medium heat. Add the onion and garlic and sauté for about 2 minutes. Don't allow them to colour. Remove from the heat and set aside to cool.

Place the cream cheese in a food processor and pulse until smooth. Add the eggs, cream, and salmon and process slowly on low speed until it's well mixed. Pour into the pan and sprinkle with the remaining Parmesan cheese.

Place the pan in a larger pan and add enough water to come halfway up the side of the pan with the cheesecake. Bake for 1 1/2 hours. Cool, then chill in the refrigerator for at least 2 hours or overnight. It slices well when chilled, but it does get firmer the longer it chills.

Quiche without a crust is like a frittata baked in a pie plate. Vary this recipe by using different kinds of low-fat cheeses or adding other vegetables, such as chopped broccoli. Cartons of cholesterol-reduced eggs are usually found next to the fresh whole eggs in the supermarket. Serves 6.

CRUSTLESS SALMON QUICHE

INGREDIENTS

1	7 1/2-oz. (213-g) can pink salmon	1
1 1/2 cups	skim milk	375 mL
1 cup	cholesterol-reduced eggs	250 mL
1/2 cup	all-purpose flour	125 mL
1 cup	grated light Cheddar cheese	250 mL
2 cups	coarsely chopped spinach, loosely packed	500 mL
1/4 cup	chopped green onions	50 mL

NUTRITION NOTES

Industry is responding to public demand for eggs with lower cholesterol. Where eggs are the primary ingredient — such as in omelettes, quiches, frittatas, and custards — cholesterol-reduced eggs provide an excellent substitute for regular eggs.

METHOD

Preheat oven to 400°F (200°C).

Drain the salmon, reserving the liquid. Crumble the salmon chunks into small pieces, crushing the bones. Set aside.

In a mixing bowl, combine the liquid from the salmon, skim milk, eggs, and flour. Beat well with an electric mixer until smooth. Pour into a greased 9 1/2-inch (24-cm) deep pie plate. Sprinkle with the salmon, cheese, spinach, and green onions. With a fork, press the solid ingredients down into the liquid mixture. Bake for 45 minutes, or until a knife inserted in the middle comes out clean. Let sit for 10 minutes before cutting.

TIMESAVER TIP

Having no crust or eggs to beat up simplifies this quiche tremendously, but for even less preparation time, buy pre-washed spinach leaves and pre-grated cheese.

The pink salmon, yellow eggs, and green herbs make this an attractive dish for a luncheon. You can use shrimp, crab, or any other kind of fish in place of salmon. Serves 4 to 6.

SALMON QUICHE
WITH DILL & PARSLEY

INGREDIENTS

1	prepared pastry shell, baked at 400°F (200°C) for 8 – 10 minutes	1
1 cup	cooked, flaked salmon, bones removed	250 mL
1/4 cup	finely chopped dill	50 mL
2 Tbsp.	finely chopped parsley	30 mL
4	large eggs	4
1/4 cup	half-and-half cream	50 mL
1/4 cup	freshly grated Parmesan cheese	50 mL
to taste	freshly ground black pepper	to taste

METHOD

Preheat oven to 350°F (180°F).

Sprinkle the salmon on the bottom of the pastry shell. Sprinkle the dill and parsley on top of the salmon.

Beat the eggs in a bowl. Add the cream and Parmesan cheese and mix together. Season with pepper and pour over the salmon and herbs in the pastry shell. Bake for 40 minutes until the custard has set.

Serve warm or cool.

Phyllo pastry transforms an ordinary meal into an elegant one. Serve with wild rice and roasted asparagus spears for a simple, but special, meal. *Serves 4.*

SALMON & ARTICHOKE HEARTS
IN PHYLLO PASTRY

INGREDIENTS

1 tsp.	olive oil	5 mL
1 cup	sliced mushrooms	250 mL
1	14-oz. (398-mL) can artichoke hearts, drained	1
1/4 tsp.	salt	1 mL
1/8 tsp	ground black pepper	.5 mL
1/4 cup	white wine	50 mL
1	small lemon, grated zest of	1
4	sheets phyllo pastry	4
1	1-lb. (500-g) salmon fillet	1
	vegetable oil spray	

NOTE

Phyllo pastry has less than 0.035 ounces (1 g) of fat per sheet — it's the butter or other fats usually spread between the layers that makes phyllo pastry rich. You can reduce the fat in most phyllo recipes and still have a tasty dish.

METHOD

Preheat oven to 375°F (190°C).

Heat the oil in a non-stick skillet over medium heat. Add the mushrooms and sauté until lightly browned. Cut the artichoke hearts into quarters and add to the mushrooms. Sauté for 1 more minute. Add the salt, pepper, wine, and lemon zest. Continue to sauté until all the liquid has evaporated. Set aside.

Place 1 sheet of phyllo pastry on a large cutting board. Spray lightly with oil. Place another sheet on top and spray with oil. Repeat with all 4 sheets.

Place the salmon fillet on top of the phyllo sheets. Spread the artichoke mixture evenly over the top of the fillet. Wrap the salmon and artichoke mixture in the pastry, tucking the ends under.

Place in a baking pan and bake for about 30 minutes, or until the salmon is done and the phyllo pastry is lightly browned. Allow 10 minutes for each inch (2.5 cm) of salmon, measured at its thickest point.

Serves 6 to 8

BOWEN ISLAND SALMON PIE

INGREDIENTS

4	8-oz. (250-g) salmon steaks, skin removed, cut in 1/2-inch (1-cm) cubes	4
8 oz.	fresh baby shrimp, peeled and cleaned	250 g
1 Tbsp.	butter	15 mL
8 oz.	fresh mushrooms, washed and sliced	250 g
1 recipe	White Sauce (see next page)	1 recipe
1	9-inch (23-cm) prepared pastry shell and top	1
1	egg yolk	1

continues on next page

METHOD

Preheat oven to 450°F (230°C).

Mix together the salmon and shrimp in a bowl. Sauté the mushrooms in butter in a skillet for 2 to 3 minutes. Fold into the salmon and shrimp mixture. Add the salmon and shrimp mixture to the white sauce and gently mix together. Put the mixture in the pastry shell and cover with the pastry top. Cut a small hole in the centre of the pastry top.

Beat the egg yolk with a whisk in a bowl. Brush the pastry top with the beaten egg yolk. Put the pastry shell on a cookie sheet. Put on the centre rack of the oven and bake for 15 minutes.

Reduce heat to 375°F (190°C) and cook for another 15 minutes, until the top is nicely browned and the pie is bubbling hot throughout. Serve at once.

White Sauce

2 Tbsp.	butter	30 mL
2 Tbsp.	all-purpose flour	30 mL
2 cups	light cream	500 mL
1 tsp.	fresh lemon juice	5 mL
1/4 tsp.	dried mustard	1 mL
pinch	dry chicken soup stock	pinch
pinch	finely chopped fresh parsley	pinch
to taste	paprika, salt, and freshly ground black pepper	to taste

White Sauce

Melt the butter in a skillet. Sprinkle with the flour and blend in, making a roux. Scald the cream in a saucepan and add cream to the roux, stirring constantly. Add the lemon juice, dried mustard, dry chicken soup stock, parsley, and paprika and blend well. Season with salt and pepper. Cook for 10 minutes, stirring occasionally.

A clever cook can impress dinner guests and use up leftover salmon with this soufflé. Serve with a green salad or fresh asparagus. Serves 4.

SALMON SOUFFLÉ WITH CHIVES

INGREDIENTS

2¹/2 Tbsp.	butter	37 mL
3 Tbsp.	all-purpose flour	45 mL
2 cups	milk	500 mL
to taste	freshly ground black pepper	to taste
2 cups	cooked salmon, bones removed	500 mL
3	eggs, separated	3
¹/4 cup	chopped chives	50 mL

METHOD

Preheat oven to 350°F (180°C).

To make the base, melt the butter in a saucepan. Add the flour, stirring constantly with a whisk to make a roux. Slowly add the milk to the saucepan and bring to a boil, stirring constantly with a whisk until the mixture thickens. Season with pepper and set aside.

Purée the salmon in a blender or food processor, then transfer to a bowl. Add the base, egg yolks, and chopped chives to the salmon and mix together well.

Beat the egg whites in a separate bowl until they are stiff. Gently fold them into the fish mixture. Put the mixture in a buttered soufflé dish in the preheated oven for 25 to 30 minutes, until the soufflé has risen and set and is light golden brown on top. Serve immediately.

SALADS

Serves 4

CANDIED SALMON & ROMAINE
WITH CLOVE MUSTARD VINAIGRETTE

INGREDIENTS

1 tsp.	minced garlic	5 mL
pinch	ground cloves (or to taste)	pinch
1 Tbsp.	sherry vinegar	15 mL
1 Tbsp.	grainy mustard	15 mL
1 tsp.	maple syrup	5 mL
1 Tbsp.	water	15 mL
1/4 cup	olive oil	50 mL
to taste	salt and black pepper	to taste
1 head	romaine lettuce	1 head
1/4 cup	candied salmon, broken in chunks	50 mL
1/4 cup	toasted croutons	50 mL

METHOD

Place the garlic, cloves, vinegar, mustard, maple syrup, and water in a mixing bowl. Drizzle in the oil, whisking constantly, until smooth and thick. Season with salt and pepper and set aside until needed.

Rinse the lettuce; rip the leaves into bite-size chunks and dry. Chill until needed.

Place the lettuce and candied salmon in a salad bowl, coat lightly with the dressing and toss well. Garnish with the croutons and serve immediately.

Serves 4

HOT SMOKED SALMON
& VEGETABLES WITH HONEY-CHILI DRESSING

INGREDIENTS

1 tsp.	minced garlic	5 mL
1 tsp.	minced ginger	5 mL
1	lime, zest and juice of	1
1 Tbsp.	honey	15 mL
1 tsp.	chili paste (or to taste)	5 mL
2 Tbsp.	light oil	30 mL
to taste	salt and black pepper	to taste
1/2 lb.	hot-smoked salmon	250 g
2 cups	sprouts (bean or sunflower)	500 mL
2 cups	shredded green cabbage	500 mL
1	red bell pepper, thinly sliced	1
to taste	salt and black pepper	to taste
for garnish	additional sprouts	for garnish
1 Tbsp.	toasted sesame seeds	15 mL

METHOD

Place the garlic, ginger, lime juice, zest, honey, and chili paste in a salad bowl. Drizzle in the oil, whisking constantly until smooth and thick. Season with salt and pepper and set aside until needed.

Add the smoked salmon, sprouts, cabbage, and red pepper to the dressing. Season with salt and pepper and toss well to mix. Garnish with a small pile of sprouts and the sesame seeds. Serve immediately.

An irreverent take on a classic — but no one seems to mind when the dressing is fatfree and there's salmon on the plate. Prawns are also an option. The bright citrus dressing really stands out when made with the trio of herbs. Use it as a marinade for chicken or single out an item from the salad and dress it up for dinner. Serves 6.

THAI SALAD NIÇOISE

INGREDIENTS

24	green beans, stemmed and trimmed	24
12 – 16	asparagus spears, trimmed	12 – 16
1 lb.	nugget potatoes, or larger potatoes quartered	500 g
4 – 6	ripe tomatoes, quartered	4 – 6
1/2	English cucumber, thinly sliced	1/2
1	red onion, halved and sliced into julienne	1
1 – 2	red bell peppers, cored and cut into julienne	1 – 2
1 1/2 lb.	salmon fillets, skin removed, cut into pieces	750 g
2 Tbsp.	olive oil	30 mL
to taste	sea salt and freshly ground black pepper	to taste

continues on next page

METHOD

Outfit a large saucepan with a steaming basket, preferably a bamboo steamer. Steam the beans and asparagus over rapidly boiling water until crisp tender, then refresh in a bowl of ice water to preserve their colour. Steam the potatoes until fork tender, replenishing the water if necessary.

Have all the cooked and fresh vegetables, except the tomatoes, prepared and ready for arranging and dressing. The tomatoes can be prepared ahead and stored in the refrigerator until needed.

Rub the salmon fillets with 1 Tbsp. (15 mL) of the olive oil and season lightly with salt and pepper. Heat the remaining 1 Tbsp. (15 mL) oil in a non-stick skillet. Sear the fillets. When nicely browned, turn them and reduce the heat to slowly cook them through. The salmon should be firm to the touch when cooked. (You can also grill or steam the salmon if you prefer.)

6	cloves garlic, finely minced	6
¼ cup	brown sugar	50 mL
2	limes, zest and juice of	2
¼ cup	nam pla (Thai fish sauce)	50 mL
1 Tbsp.	sambal oelek (Thai hot sauce)	15 mL
1 cup	chopped cilantro, mint, basil or a combination	250 mL

Arrange the vegetables on a large platter or individual plates. Top with the salmon fillets. Whisk together the garlic, sugar, lime zest and juice, nam pla, sambal oelek, and herbs. The dressing may be made ahead, but the herbs should be added just before serving to avoid darkening. Spoon the fresh dressing over the platter or pass it in small bowls to each dinner guest.

This salad is best served soon after it's mixed with the dressing so that the roasted skins stay crispy. The smoked salmon makes it deluxe. If you don't have smoked salmon, add 1/2 cup (125 mL) freshly grated Parmesan cheese instead. If you plan to take it on a picnic, which you should, bring the dressing separately in a little jar and toss the potatoes with the dressing just before serving. Serves 4.

ROASTED BABY RED POTATO SALAD
WITH SMOKED SALMON

INGREDIENTS

1 1/4 lb.	baby red potatoes, quartered	625 g
1 Tbsp.	olive oil, for salad	15 mL
1/4 tsp.	salt	1 mL
12 oz.	green beans, cut into 2-inch (5-cm) pieces	375 g
1/2	small red onion, thinly sliced	1/2
1/4 cup	sliced chives or green onion	50 mL
3 1/2 oz.	smoked salmon, sliced in strips	100 g
1 1/2 Tbsp.	red wine vinegar	22 mL
1 1/2 Tbsp.	Dijon mustard	22 mL
1/4 tsp.	salt	1 mL
1/2 tsp.	freshly ground black pepper	2 mL
5 Tbsp.	olive oil, for dressing	75 mL

METHOD

Preheat oven to 375°F (190°C).

Toss the potatoes in the 1 Tbsp. (15 mL) olive oil and season with the salt. Spread the potatoes on a baking sheet and bake for about 30 minutes, or until soft. Cool. Blanch the green beans in boiling water for 1 minute, drain, and plunge into ice water to stop the cooking and fix the colour. Drain well.

Combine the potatoes, green beans, red onion, chives or green onion, and smoked salmon in a bowl.

Whisk together the red wine vinegar, Dijon mustard, salt, and pepper in a small bowl. Slowly drizzle in the 5 Tbsp. (75 mL) olive oil while continuing to whisk. Just before serving, toss the salad with the dressing.

Serve this great main-course salad for lunch, along with fresh crusty rolls and a lemon sorbet for dessert. Any type of canned salmon can be used, but red sockeye salmon gives the salad extra colour. Serves 4.

SALMON SALAD

INGREDIENTS

1	7¹/2-oz. (213-g) can sockeye salmon	1
1 Tbsp.	Dijon mustard	15 mL
1 Tbsp.	olive oil	15 mL
2 Tbsp.	apple juice	30 mL
2 Tbsp.	apple cider vinegar	30 mL
1	clove garlic, crushed	1
to taste	salt and ground black pepper	to taste
1	head butter lettuce	1
1	head red leaf lettuce	1
1	tomato, diced	1
1	carrot, grated	1

METHOD

Drain the salmon, reserving the liquid, and set aside.

Combine the liquid from the canned salmon with the mustard, oil, juice, vinegar, garlic, salt, and pepper. Shake or whisk together well.

To prepare the salad, tear the butter lettuce and red leaf lettuce into bite-size pieces. Place in a large salad bowl. Add the diced tomato and grated carrot. Crumble the salmon over the vegetables.

Pour the dressing over the salad and toss.

TIMESAVER TIP

Use pre-packaged salad greens instead of the lettuces. Mesclun mix is especially delicious.

Asparagus is the harbinger of spring and warm sunny days. I start buying it as soon as the first bunches show up in the market, ignoring the exorbitant price. If the nut vinaigrette is too rich for you, substitute your favourite dressing instead. Serves 6.

SPRING ASPARAGUS, SALMON
& HAZELNUT SALAD

INGREDIENTS

1 lb.	young fresh asparagus	500 g
1	bunch fresh spinach or mesclun	1
6	5-oz. (150-g) salmon fillets	6
1/4 cup	hazelnuts, toasted, skinned, and coarsely chopped	50 mL

Hazelnut Vinaigrette
Makes about 1 1/4 cups (300 mL)

1/4 cup	hazelnuts, toasted, skinned, and chopped	50 mL
1 Tbsp.	puréed fresh ginger	15 mL
2 Tbsp.	minced lemon thyme	30 mL
1 Tbsp.	smooth Dijon mustard	15 mL
1	lime, juice and zest of	1
1/4 cup	honey	50 mL
1/4 cup	sherry vinegar	50 mL
1/3 cup	canola oil	75 mL
to taste	salt and hot chili flakes	to taste

METHOD

Wash the asparagus, snapping off and discarding the brittle ends. Wash the greens, drying them well to allow the dressing to stick. Place the salmon on a baking sheet, skin-side down, and sprinkle the hazelnuts over the top.

Preheat oven to 450°F (230°C).

Roast the salmon until tender and flaky, about 10 minutes.

Steam the asparagus, toss it in a little dressing, and arrange it on plates. Toss the greens in 3/4 cup (175 mL) of the vinaigrette and arrange them next to the asparagus. Place a salmon fillet on each plate and serve hot.

Hazelnut Vinaigrette

Whisk together all the ingredients. Store in the refrigerator until needed. If you plan to keep this dressing more than 1 day, add the chopped nuts just before using the dressing to keep them from going soft.

Serves 6

SAYONARA SALMON

INGREDIENTS

1	16-oz. (454-g) package rice sticks	1
	canola oil for frying	
6	6-oz. (175-g) fillets Atlantic salmon	6
1	lemon, zest of	1
1 Tbsp.	grated fresh ginger	15 mL
1 Tbsp.	minced cilantro	15 mL
to taste	hot chili flakes	to taste
2 tsp.	canola oil	10 mL
2 Tbsp.	minced pickled ginger	30 mL

METHOD

Open the rice stick package inside a large paper bag to control the mess. Break the rice sticks into manageable lengths with your hands. Heat 1 inch (2.5 cm) canola oil in a large skillet and set a wire rack on a baking sheet close by. Using chopsticks or tongs, test the temperature of the oil by immersing 1 strand of a rice stick. If it immediately puffs up, the oil is hot enough. When the

METHOD — continued

oil is hot, pick up a handful of rice sticks with tongs or chopsticks and immerse in the hot oil, keeping the tongs or chopsticks in place. When the rice sticks are puffed, place them on the rack to drain. Repeat with the remaining rice sticks. Let stand, uncovered and at room temperature, until needed, then heap them on individual plates.

Sprinkle the salmon with the lemon zest, ginger, cilantro, and hot chili flakes. Pan-steam the salmon in the oil over low heat in a non-stick saucepan. Use a lid that fits snugly over the salmon inside the saucepan. Turn the salmon frequently and reduce the heat if it sizzles or browns. After 7 to 10 minutes, or when the salmon is cooked through, place each piece on top of the crisp rice sticks and garnish with the pickled ginger.

Tart smoky tomato vinaigrette, creamy goat cheese, and sweet balsamic syrup combine to highlight the flavours of warm salmon. When selecting your ingredients, look for salmon that's firm and deep red. Choose tomatoes that are ripe, but not too soft — they need to hold up during grilling. The vinaigrette, syrup, and quenelles can be made ahead so all you need to do at serving time is grill the salmon and assemble the salad. Serves 4.

ALDER-SMOKED SALMON SALAD
WITH FIRE-GRILLED TOMATO VINAIGRETTE & BALSAMIC SYRUP

INGREDIENTS

1/2 cup + 2 tsp.	balsamic vinegar	125 mL + 10 mL
2	medium tomatoes	2
3/4 tsp.	olive oil	4 mL
1	shallot, finely diced	1
1	clove garlic, minced	1
1/4 cup	olive oil	50 mL
3 Tbsp.	canola oil	45 mL
3 Tbsp.	red wine vinegar	45 mL
1/2 tsp.	sea salt	2 mL
1/2 tsp.	freshly ground black pepper	2 mL
6 oz.	fresh goat cheese	175 g
4	4-oz. (125-g) pieces salmon	4
4 cups	mesclun greens	1 L
4	stalks chives	4

METHOD

Place the 1/2 cup (125 mL) balsamic vinegar in a small saucepan over medium heat and bring to a boil. Reduce the heat and simmer for about 5 minutes or until it's reduced to 3 Tbsp. (45 mL). Remove from the heat and set aside to cool.

Preheat the barbecue to low and soak a handful of alder chips in water for 10 minutes.

Cut the tomatoes in half crosswise, squeeze out and discard the seeds, and place the tomatoes in a small mixing bowl. Toss them in the 3/4 tsp. (4 mL) olive oil and place them on the grill for 3 minutes per side. Remove and cool. While the tomatoes are cooling, combine the shallot, garlic, 1/4 cup (50 mL) olive oil, canola oil, red wine vinegar, balsamic vinegar, salt, and pepper in a small bowl. Dice the grilled tomatoes and add to the vinaigrette. Stir just to combine.

Use two teaspoons to form $1/2$ oz. (14 g) of soft goat cheese into an oval. Repeat, making 3 quenelles per plate. You could also simply crumble the cheese over the finished salad.

Grill the salmon pieces on the barbecue over medium heat for about 3 minutes per side or until firm to the touch. Divide the mesclun greens among 4 plates and place the grilled salmon on top. Drizzle the tomato vinaigrette over the salmon and greens. Place the quenelles at three points around each salad. Drizzle balsamic syrup around the perimeter. Cut the chives in half and place criss-crossed over the salmon. Serve immediately.

Serves 4 to 6

BOW PASTA & SPINACH
WITH CREAMY SMOKED SALMON DRESSING

INGREDIENTS

6 cups	water	1.5 L
1 tsp.	salt	5 mL
2 cups	bow pasta	500 mL
1 tsp.	olive oil	5 mL
	additional olive oil for drizzling	
4 cups	washed baby spinach leaves	1 L
1/4 cup	shredded smoked salmon	50 mL
1 Tbsp.	capers	15 mL

Creamy Smoked Salmon Dressing

1	lemon, juice and zest of	1
2 Tbsp.	sour cream	30 mL
2 Tbsp.	mayonnaise	30 mL
2 Tbsp.	water	30 mL
1/4 cup	chopped smoked salmon	50 mL
1 tsp.	capers	5 mL
2 Tbsp.	olive oil	30 mL
to taste	salt and black pepper	to taste

METHOD

Bring the water and salt to a rolling boil and stir in the pasta and oil. Bring back to a boil and cook until *al dente*, about 7 to 8 minutes. If it foams, reduce the heat to medium-high. Drain and shake the pasta free of excess water. Drizzle with a little oil and toss well. Transfer to a baking sheet and spread out evenly. Cool to room temperature and toss lightly to separate.

Place the cooked pasta and spinach in a large salad bowl. Add the dressing and toss well to coat. Sprinkle with the salmon and capers and serve immediately.

Creamy Smoked Salmon Dressing

Place the lemon juice, zest, sour cream, mayonnaise, water, smoked salmon, capers, and oil in a blender. Process until smooth and season lightly with salt and well with pepper. Thin with a little water, if necessary, to make a pouring consistency. Chill until needed.

SALMON CARPACCIO WITH MUSHROOM SALAD & SHAVED PARMESAN | page 61

Karen Barnaby — *Screamingly Good Food*

Bill Jones

SALMON & CHIVE FISH CAKES | page 74

Noël Richardson — *Summer Delights*

SMOKED SOCKEYE SALMON CHEESECAKE | page 78

Dan Atkinson — *Salmon House on the Hill*

Cooking alters the texture of cold-smoked salmon for the worse, so don't be tempted to cook it, however briefly!
The nasturtium blossoms add a peppery note that contrasts well with the smoked salmon. Serve this salad
warm or cool the noodles completely before combining the ingredients. Serves 6.

LINGUINI WITH HERBS

& COLD-SMOKED SALMON

INGREDIENTS		
1/2	small zucchini, finely diced	1/2
1/2	red bell pepper, finely diced	1/2
3 – 4	green onions, sliced finely on a diagonal	3 – 4
2 Tbsp.	minced fresh parsley	30 mL
1 Tbsp.	minced fresh thyme	15 mL
1	lemon, zest and juice of	1
1 Tbsp.	hazelnut oil or extra virgin olive oil	15 mL
2 – 4 oz.	cold-smoked salmon, finely sliced	50 – 125 g
to taste	salt and freshly cracked pepper	to taste
1 1/2 lb.	dried linguini	750 g
1/2 cup	sunflower or mustard sprouts	125 mL
12	nasturtium blossoms (optional)	12

METHOD

Toss the zucchini, red pepper, green onions, parsley, thyme, lemon zest and juice, and oil with the salmon. Season with salt and pepper.

Bring a large pot of salted water to a boil and cook the linguini until it's *al dente*, about 8 minutes. Drain and cool under cold running water. Toss the pasta with the salmon mixture. Add the sprouts and serve, garnishing each plate with nasturtium blossoms if using.

Kikkoman memmi is a bottled sauce base that's combined with water to make a broth. Soba noodles are made from buckwheat flour. The pickled ginger I use is in short julienne strips and a dark pink. It's saltier and crunchier than the sweet pickled ginger used with sushi. Everything in this dish is available at Japanese and well-stocked Asian grocery stores. Serves 2.

CHILLED SOBA NOODLES
WITH SALMON

INGREDIENTS

½ cup	Kikkoman memmi	125 mL
2 cups	water	500 mL
½	1-lb. (500-g) package soba noodles	½
2	6-oz. (175-g) salmon fillets	2
to taste	salt	to taste
for garnish	English cucumber, julienne strips	for garnish
for garnish	pickled ginger	for garnish
for garnish	sliced green onions	for garnish
for garnish	toasted sesame seeds	for garnish
to serve	wasabi	to serve

METHOD

Mix together the Kikkoman memmi and the water. Set aside.

Soba noodles require a special cooking technique to give them their desirable bouncy texture. Half-fill a large saucepan with cold water and bring to a boil. Drop the soba noodles into the water, a few at a time, in a continuous stream. When the water returns to a boil, add 1 cup (250 mL) cold water. When it comes to a boil again, add another cup (250 mL) cold water. Continue as above, checking the noodles frequently. When they are tender but firm, drain, and rinse them under cold water. Place in two large bowls.

While the noodles are cooking, turn on the broiler and sprinkle 2 salmon fillets liberally with salt. Place the salmon skin-side up on a pan and broil close to the heat. I like salmon medium-rare, cooked on 1 side only. If you don't share my sentiment, turn the fish over and cook it through.

Place the salmon on top of the noodles. Pour the memmi broth around the noodles. Place English cucumber and a little pickled ginger on top of the salmon. Sprinkle sliced green onions and toasted sesame seeds over everything. Serve with wasabi on the side, to stir into the broth as desired.

BARBECUE

The down-to-earth flavours of rich sockeye and wild mushrooms are fabulous with the light floral butter. Edible flower blossoms are readily available throughout the summer months from specialty herb suppliers. For this recipe I buy a mixed variety of blossoms and pick the petals off by hand. Serves 4.

ALDER-GRILLED SOCKEYE SALMON
WITH SUMMER BLOSSOM BUTTER & SAUTÉED CHANTERELLES

INGREDIENTS

4	7-oz. (200-g) sockeye salmon fillets	4
2 Tbsp.	extra virgin olive oil	30 mL
to taste	sea salt and freshly ground black pepper	to taste
2 cups	fresh chanterelle mushrooms	500 mL
1/4 cup	chicken stock	50 mL
1 tsp.	chopped fresh basil	5 mL
1 tsp.	chopped fresh parsley	5 mL
1 tsp.	fresh thyme	5 mL
2 Tbsp.	butter	30 mL
4 slices	Summer Blossom Butter	4 slices

continues on next page

METHOD

Preheat the barbecue to hot and scatter the pre-soaked alder wood chips over the coals (optional).

Brush the salmon fillets with the olive oil and season with salt and pepper. Grill the salmon for about 4 minutes per side or until firm to the touch.

In a large skillet over medium heat, cook the mushrooms with the chicken stock, basil, parsley, and thyme for 3 to 4 minutes, or until the mushrooms are tender and most of the liquid is gone. Add the butter, salt, and pepper, then cook for another 2 minutes.

To serve, divide the warm sautéed chanterelles among 4 plates. Place a sockeye fillet over each mound of mushrooms. Slice 4 rounds of blossom butter, about 3/8 inch (1 cm) thick, and place 1 on each piece of salmon. The heat from the salmon should be just enough to begin to melt the butter.

Summer Blossom Butter
Makes 1 cup (250 mL)

8 oz.	butter, softened	250 g
1 cup	edible flower petals (nasturtium, rose, calendula, chive, etc.)	250 mL
1 Tbsp.	minced garlic	15 mL
2 Tbsp.	fresh lemon juice	30 mL
1 Tbsp.	chopped fresh parsley	15 mL

Summer Blossom Butter

Using a wooden spoon, mix all the ingredients together in a small bowl until well combined. Lay out 2 sheets of plastic wrap about 18 inches (45 cm) long, 1 on top of the other. Place the butter on the plastic in a log shape and roll it up. Twist 1 end of the roll and tie it tightly with string. Twist the other end until it's quite tight and the roll is firm to the touch, then tie it as well. Chill for at least 2 hours before using. Freeze unused portions.

Serves 6

PIQUANT GRILLED SALMON

WITH RISOTTO FILLED PEPPERS

INGREDIENTS

2 Tbsp.	olive oil	30 mL
1 1/2 cups	tomato juice	375 mL
2	cloves garlic, split in half	2
1	small Spanish onion, cut into brunoise	1
1 cup	Arborio or other risotto rice	250 mL
3 Tbsp.	grated Parmigiano Reggiano	45 mL
1 Tbsp.	chopped parsley	15 mL
1 Tbsp.	finely chopped chives	15 mL
6	small sweet peppers (cubanelle, Anaheim, etc.)	6
6	fresh salmon fillets	6
2	green chilies, finely chopped	2
to taste	coarse salt	to taste

METHOD

Heat the oil in a large skillet. In a saucepan, warm the tomato juice.

Add the garlic and onion to the hot oil. Sauté without browning for 5 minutes. Add the rice and continue to sauté for another 5 minutes. Add the tomato juice gradually, stirring continually, until all the liquid is absorbed by the rice. Add water or stock if necessary until rice is tender. Stir in the grated cheese, parsley, and chives. Remove from the heat.

Cut the stems from the 6 peppers and use a paring knife to remove the pith and seeds. Stuff the peppers with the risotto mixture. Place the peppers in a large skillet with enough tomato juice to cover the bottom of the skillet. Cover and set aside.

Preheat oven to 350°F (175°C).

Rub the salmon fillets with the chopped chilies and sprinkle liberally with coarse salt. Five minutes before you plan to start grilling the salmon, place the covered pan of stuffed peppers in the oven. When the peppers are almost cooked, grill the salmon on the barbecue for about 3 minutes per side or to desired doneness.

To serve, warm 6 plates. Slice each pepper and arrange the slices in an overlapping fan pattern, 1 pepper per plate. Place a fillet of cooked salmon beside each pepper. Spoon some of the cooking liquid from the pepper pan onto each plate. Serve immediately.

Serves 6

BARBECUED SALMON
WITH OLIVE RISSOLE & TOMATOES

INGREDIENTS

2	medium potatoes, cooked and peeled	2
3 Tbsp.	pitted Nicoise or Spanish olives	45 mL
3 Tbsp.	roasted red peppers	45 mL
1	clove garlic, finely chopped	1
1/4 cup	olive oil for cooking	50 mL
3 Tbsp.	diced ripe tomato	45 mL
to taste	salt and freshly ground black pepper	to taste
6	5-oz. (150-g) fillets fresh salmon, at room temperature	6
to taste	salt	to taste
1/2 tsp.	chopped fresh chilies	2 mL
2 Tbsp.	fresh lemon juice	30 mL
1 tsp.	fresh summer savoury leaves	5 mL

METHOD

Preheat oven to 400°F (200°C).

Dice the cooked potatoes. Dice the olives, peppers, and tomatoes to a uniform size. Sauté the garlic in an oven-proof skillet with 2 Tbsp. (30 mL) of the olive oil. Add the potatoes and place in the oven for 10 minutes. When the potatoes are golden brown, add the olives and the peppers. Return to the oven for 10 more minutes, stirring occasionally.

Meanwhile, season the salmon with salt and the chilies. Heat a skillet on high heat and add the remaining 2 Tbsp. (30 mL) of olive oil. Sear the salmon for 2 minutes on each side and then place in the oven to finish cooking, about 5 minutes.

To serve, warm 6 dinner plates. Place a salmon fillet on each plate. Sprinkle each fillet with lemon juice. Stir the tomato and the summer savoury into the rissole vegetables. Place a mound of rissole beside each salmon fillet. Serve immediately.

Serves 6

CHILI & ROCK SALT
GRILLED SALMON

INGREDIENTS

6	6-oz. (175-g) fresh salmon fillets	6
to taste	coarse-grained salt	to taste
1	green chili, seeded and finely chopped	1

METHOD

Prepare a charcoal or gas barbecue.

Purée the chili and salt in a food processor.

Coat the fillets of salmon with the chili paste. Wait until the barbecue has burned down to a nice slow fire or set the gas barbecue to low heat. Place the fillets of salmon, skin-side down, on the grill. Grill until each side is golden brown, about 7 minutes per side. Serve with steamed new potatoes and asparagus.

Sorrel and salmon is a traditional combination in the French culinary repertoire, and I often wonder if some classic sauces arose out of the sorrel bush's unfailing generosity of production. I know I sometimes go out and pick some just because it's so prolific! The wood chips should soak for an hour, which allows just enough time to make the sorrel-spinach sauce, apply the rub to the fish, and let it cure. Serves 4.

GRILLED SALMON

WITH SORREL-SPINACH SAUCE

INGREDIENTS

4	5-oz. (150-g) salmon fillets	4
4 Tbsp.	fresh tarragon	50 mL
2 tsp.	cracked fennel seed	10 mL
to taste	freshly cracked pepper	to taste
1	lime, zest of	1
1 tsp.	mustard seed	5 mL
1 Tbsp.	olive oil	15 mL
1 cup	Sorrel-Spinach Sauce (page 109)	250 mL
for garnish	chive blossoms	for garnish

continues on next page

Place the salmon fillets in a shallow pan. Combine all ingredients except for the sorrel-spinach sauce and chive blossoms, and smear onto the flesh side of the salmon. Marinate at room temperature for 30 minutes.

Preheat the grill to medium.

Lightly oil the grill and cook until the fish is just done, between 7 and 10 minutes, depending on the thickness. Turn when two-thirds done if desired, or cook entirely skin-side down.

If you're using wood chips for smoke, drain them and place on one side only of the grill, on the lava rocks and under the bars, with the heat set at low on that side. Place the fish on the other side of the grill, over medium heat. Close the lid and don't peek. Wait until 5 to 7 minutes elapse before looking.

Serve the grilled salmon on a pool of Sorrel-Spinach Sauce with a chive blossom or two for garnish.

Sorrel-Spinach Sauce

Makes about 3 cups (750 mL)

1 bunch	spinach	1 bunch
1 bunch	sorrel	1 bunch
2	shallots	2
1 tsp.	unsalted butter	5 mL
1/2 cup	dry white wine	125 mL
1	lemon, zest only	1
1/2 tsp.	cracked fennel seeds	2 mL
2 Tbsp.	minced fresh thyme, tarragon, or lemon thyme	30 mL
2	green onions, minced	2
2 cups	buttermilk	500 mL
to taste	salt and hot chili flakes	to taste

Sorrel-Spinach Sauce

Wash the spinach and sorrel, discarding the stems. Don't spin dry. In a sauté pan, sauté the shallots in the butter, cooking until tender, without browning. Add the wine, bring to a boil, and add the spinach, turning the leaves with tongs until they just wilt.

Remove to a food processor and purée finely, along with the sorrel leaves. Add remaining ingredients, thinning to the desired consistency with buttermilk. Adjust the flavours and serve cold.

NOTE

The Sorrel-Spinach Sauce makes a refreshing cold summer soup as well as a dip for crudités, a pasta sauce, especially when partnered with poached shrimp on linguini, or a tart, lean sauce to layer with sweet potatoes and Yukon Golds for an end-of-summer gratin.

This salmon preparation is most often cooked on a barbecue, but it also works well in the oven. Either way, the cedar gives the salmon an inviting, slightly smoky taste. Serve it with corn on the cob, steamed new potatoes, and green beans. Serves 4.

CEDAR PLANK SALMON

INGREDIENTS

2 Tbsp.	olive oil	30 mL
1/2	lemon, juice of	1/2
1 Tbsp.	brown sugar	15 mL
1 Tbsp.	chopped fresh dill or parsley	15 mL
to taste	salt and black pepper	to taste
4	6-oz. (175-g) salmon fillets, skin on	4
for garnish	lemon slices	for garnish

ERIC'S OPTIONS

Use an equal amount of maple syrup or honey instead of brown sugar. For pepper-crusted cedar plank salmon, coat the fish with a generous amount of coarsely cracked black pepper before cooking.

CEDAR PLANKS

Untreated cedar planks are available at many supermarkets. You can also find them at lumber supply stores.

METHOD

Pre-soak an untreated cedar plank by submerging it in cold water for 2 hours.

Place the oil, lemon juice, sugar, dill or parsley, salt, and pepper in a bowl and mix well. Add the salmon and turn to coat. Marinate for 30 minutes.

Remove the plank from the water and dry the side the fish will be placed on. If you're using the oven, pre-heat it to 425°F (220°C). Place the fish on the plank and bake for 15 to 20 minutes, or until just cooked through. If using the barbecue, preheat it to medium-high. If you have a two-burner barbecue, turn one side off and lower the other to medium-low. Set the fish on the plank and place on the unlit side of the barbecue. (If you have a one-burner barbecue, set to its lowest setting.) Close the lid and cook for 15 to 20 minutes, or until the fish is cooked through. Keep a spray bottle handy in case the board ignites on the bottom. Set the plank on a serving tray and garnish with lemon slices.

This is what results when a person grows up in more than one region of North America. The cedar or alder plank is a West Coast native way of cooking salmon, and the mustard glaze is inspired by the acres of fresh mustard that add a yellow floral note to the patchwork of crops across the Prairies. Serves 6 to 8.

CEDAR PLANKED SALMON
WITH HONEY & MUSTARD

INGREDIENTS

3 Tbsp.	canola oil	45 mL
1	3-lb. (1.5-kg) piece of salmon, skin on	1
1/2 cup	honey	125 mL
4 Tbsp.	mustard	50 mL
1	lemon, zest of	1
4 Tbsp.	minced fresh thyme or sage	50 mL
to taste	hot chili flakes	to taste
to taste	salt	to taste
for garnish	lemon, cut in wedges	for garnish
for garnish	sprigs of thyme or sage	for garnish

NOTE

Use an oven or your outdoor grill, and be sure the wood is unsprayed and pesticide-free. If you can't be sure, don't use it. If you're grilling, treat the plank or shingle like wood chips, and soak it well to minimize flaming.

METHOD

Preheat oven to 450°F (230°C) or heat the grill to medium-high.

Brush the wood with the oil and lay the fish skin-side down on the wood. Mix together the honey, mustard, lemon zest, minced herbs, hot chili flakes, and salt.

Brush the exposed surfaces of the fish with half the glaze, then transfer to the oven or the grill. Don't over-cook: allow about 7 minutes per inch (2.5 cm) of thickness. If you're uncertain, use a small sharp knife to separate several flakes at the thickest part — when done, it should no longer be transparent, but opaque.

Remove the fish from the heat and brush with the remaining glaze. Serve from the board. Garnish with lemon wedges and sprigs of fresh thyme or sage.

Millet is a little yellow grain most often relegated to bird feed. But toasted and simply steamed it has a lovely nutty flavour that works perfectly with a pot of Asian greens. The simple soy-glazed salmon makes a perfect counterpoint to this unique grain dish. Look for millet in health-food stores. Serves 4.

GRILLED SALMON
WITH SWEET SOY GLAZE & MILLET HOT POT

INGREDIENTS

4	5-oz. (150-g) boneless salmon fillet pieces, skin on	4
	canola oil	
to taste	salt and white pepper	to taste
2 Tbsp.	butter	30 mL
2 Tbsp.	honey	30 mL
2 Tbsp.	dark soy sauce	30 mL
1/4 tsp.	hot Asian chili paste	1 mL
2 tsp.	oyster sauce	10 mL

continues on next page

METHOD

For presentation, cut each portion of fish into 2 pieces. Rub the skin side of the fish with a little canola oil to prevent it from sticking to the grill. Season the flesh side with salt and white pepper. Set aside.

Heat the butter, honey, and soy sauce together in a small saucepan. Simmer until smooth and thick. Stir in the chili paste and oyster sauce, and let cool.

Brush the flesh side of the salmon liberally with the sauce. Preheat the barbecue to medium-high heat and brush the grill with canola oil. Place the fish, skin-side down, on the grill. Cover the barbecue and cook until the fish is barely cooked through, about 10 minutes per inch (2.5 cm) thickness. Brush the fish with more sauce 2 or 3 times during cooking.

To serve, place a mound of millet and vegetables in each of 4 shallow rimmed soup bowls, and arrange 2 pieces of grilled salmon over each portion.

Millet Hot Pot

Serves 4

Millet Hot Pot

3/4 cup	hulled millet seeds	175 mL
2 Tbsp.	vegetable oil	30 mL
2	cloves garlic, minced	2
2 tsp.	minced fresh ginger	10 mL
2 cups	chopped gai lan (Chinese broccoli)	500 mL
6	baby bok choy, stems sliced and leaves shredded and reserved	6
1	red bell pepper, seeded and chopped	1
1 Tbsp.	Indonesian sweet soy sauce (kecap manis) or teriyaki sauce	15 mL
1 1/2 cups	chicken stock	375 mL
1 tsp.	hot chili sauce	5 mL
4	green onions, cut into 2-inch (5-cm) pieces	4
1 tsp.	sesame oil	5 mL
2 Tbsp.	chopped Thai basil or fresh mint	30 mL
1/4 cup	coarsely chopped roasted cashews	50 mL

Stir the millet in a large dry skillet over medium-high heat until the seeds are golden and begin to pop, about 5 minutes. Remove from the heat and set aside.

Heat the oil in a wok or saucepan over medium-high heat and stir-fry the garlic and ginger together for 30 seconds. Add the gai lan, bok choy stems, and red pepper and stir-fry for 2 minutes. Cover and steam for another 2 minutes.

Stir in the soy sauce, chicken stock, and chili sauce and bring to a boil. Add the toasted millet, then cover the saucepan, reduce the heat to low, and simmer for 15 to 20 minutes.

Remove from the heat and stir in the reserved bok choy leaves and the green onions. Let the saucepan stand, covered, for another 10 minutes to steam the millet.

Fluff the millet with a fork and stir in the sesame oil and basil or mint. Sprinkle with cashew nuts.

I learned this technique one summer while working as a cook in a sports fishing camp on the central coast of B.C. In the last few years, I've introduced it to many students and customers, who have responded with rave reviews. Here I pair it with a delicious compound butter. *Serves 6.*

SWEET BBQ SALMON,
RIVERS INLET STYLE

INGREDIENTS

1/4 cup	brown sugar	50 mL
2 Tbsp.	coarse salt	30 mL
1/2 tsp.	dried mustard	2 mL
2 1/2 lb.	salmon fillets, skin removed	1.1 kg

Sun-Dried Tomato, Caper & Dill Butter
Makes one 3-inch (8-cm) log

2 Tbsp.	very finely chopped sun-dried tomatoes	30 mL
2 tsp.	finely chopped capers	10 mL
1 Tbsp.	finely chopped dill	15 mL
5 Tbsp.	unsalted butter, room temperature	75 mL

NOTE

When grilling a large, thick chunk of salmon, you can leave the skin on and grill it skin-side up for a few minutes to mark the salmon nicely with grill marks, then turn it over and complete the cooking with the skin-side down. The skin will become charred and will separate easily. The salmon can be lifted off, leaving the skin behind.

METHOD

Mix together the brown sugar, salt, and dried mustard. Sprinkle onto both sides of the salmon fillets. Marinate in a non-reactive dish for 4 to 5 hours, turning occasionally. The next step is very important: rinse the salmon well under cold running water.

Preheat the barbecue or grill and oil lightly.

Grill the salmon for about 4 minutes per side or until the fish is barely firm. Just before serving, unwrap the chilled compound butter and cut into 1/2 -inch (1-cm) nuggets. Place on the hot fish and serve.

Sun-Dried Tomato, Caper & Dill Butter

Place all the ingredients in a small bowl and beat very well with a wooden spoon. Scrape the mixture onto a piece of wax paper or parchment. Fold the paper over the mixture and roll up into a 3-inch (8-cm) tube. Chill well.

BAKED & BROILED

Delicious if grilled instead of oven-roasted, this entrée is easy to prepare and spans all seasons. The cabbage component isn't mushy à la boiled cabbage, but is instead a just-softened dish lightened with wine and lemon. Serves 6.

OVEN-ROASTED SALMON

WITH MAPLE MUSTARD GLAZE & PANCETTA BRAISED CABBAGE

INGREDIENTS

6	6-oz. (175-g) fresh boneless salmon fillets	6
to taste	salt and pepper	to taste
2 Tbsp.	coarse-grained mustard	30 mL
2 Tbsp.	maple syrup	30 mL
2	green onions, chopped	2
1 tsp.	chopped fresh tarragon	5 mL
3	slices pancetta (or bacon), diced	3
2	shallots, chopped	2
1/3	head Savoy cabbage, thinly sliced	1/3
1/2 cup	white wine	125 mL
2 Tbsp.	fresh lemon juice	30 mL
2 Tbsp.	honey	30 mL
1 tsp.	chopped fresh thyme	5 mL

METHOD

Preheat oven to 375°F (190°C). Place the salmon on a baking sheet lined with foil or parchment paper. Season with salt and pepper.

In a bowl, stir together the mustard, maple syrup, green onions, and tarragon to make the mustard glaze. Season to taste and set aside.

Brush fillets generously with mustard glaze and place in the oven. Cook until fish flakes when touched with a fork or to desired doneness, about 8 minutes. Use remaining glaze as a sauce and drizzle over cooked salmon.

Cook the pancetta in a large skillet over medium-high heat. Remove from the heat and drain off some but not all of the fat.

Add the shallots and cabbage to the pancetta and toss in the skillet for 1 minute. Add the white wine, lemon juice, honey, and thyme and continue tossing the cabbage until just soft, about 4 minutes. Season to taste. Serve salmon warm on top of a bed of cabbage.

This recipe is great for crowds because the glaze can be made in advance and the salmon pieces prepared ahead of time and cooked at the last minute. Even the least adventurous seem to enjoy the sweet and sour heat the glaze gives to the salmon. This goes wonderfully with grilled vegetables and a simple couscous salad. Serves 6.

ROASTED SALMON FILLETS
WITH HONEY CHILI GLAZE

INGREDIENTS

6	6-oz. (175-g) salmon fillets	6
1/2 cup	butter, melted	125 mL
1/2 cup	honey	125 mL
1/4 cup	hot sauce (or to taste)	50 mL
to taste	salt and freshly ground black pepper	to taste

METHOD

Preheat oven to 450°F (230°C).

Place the salmon on a baking tray skin-side down. Combine the butter, honey, and hot sauce, and brush over the salmon. Refrigerate until the glaze has set. This can be done up to 8 hours ahead.

Just before baking, salt and pepper the salmon. Bake for about 8 minutes (2 minutes less if the salmon pieces are thin and 2 minutes more if they're really thick). Remove from the oven and serve immediately or at room temperature.

OPTIONAL

Try adding chopped peaches or chopped mangos to the glaze.

The salmon steams inside the banana leaf and the fish juices combine with the flavouring ingredients to create a unique sauce. Any firm-fleshed fish (such as halibut) can be substituted for salmon. You can prepare the packages up to 1 hour ahead of cooking. *Serves 4.*

SALMON BAKED

IN BANANA LEAVES

INGREDIENTS

4 tsp.	Red Curry Paste (see next page)	20 mL
1/2 cup	coconut cream (the thick top portion of canned coconut milk)	125 mL
2 Tbsp.	palm or brown sugar	30 mL
1 Tbsp.	fish sauce	15 mL
1/2 cup	sliced basil leaves	125 mL
8	kaffir lime leaves, finely sliced, or 1 Tbsp. (15 mL) lime zest	8
4	6-oz. (175-g) salmon fillets	4
4	frozen banana leaves, about 12 x 14 inches (30 x 35 cm), defrosted	4

continues on next page

METHOD

Preheat oven to 375°F (190°C).

Mix together the curry paste, coconut cream, sugar, fish sauce, basil, and lime leaves. Coat each salmon fillet with the mixture. Place each coated fillet on a banana leaf. Fold the leaf to completely enclose the salmon. Pin together with toothpicks.

Place the packages on a cookie sheet and bake for about 15 minutes.

BANANA LEAVES

The large flexible leaves of the banana plant are used throughout Asia to wrap foods for grilling, steaming, or baking. They keep the food moist and impart a subtle, herblike flavour. To use banana leaves, remove the thick central stalk, rinse the leaves well and use as is or blanch them in boiling water for a few seconds to soften them. They are often for sale in the West in the freezer section of Vietnamese, Indian, or Philippine markets. Aluminum foil or parchment paper can be used instead.

Red Curry Paste

Makes about 1 cup (250 mL)

15	dried hot chili peppers	15
1	2-inch (5-cm) cube fresh galanga root	1
2	stalks lemon grass	2
2 Tbsp.	coriander seeds	30 mL
2 Tbsp.	cumin seeds	30 mL
4 tsp.	paprika	20 mL
1/4 tsp.	turmeric	1 mL
1/4 tsp.	cinnamon	1 mL
3	1/2-inch (1-cm) pieces lime zest, finely chopped	3
6	shallots (or 1/2 onion), chopped	6
5	cilantro roots, cleaned and diced (or 10 stems)	5
6	cloves garlic, chopped	6
1 1/2 tsp.	shrimp paste	7 mL
pinch	salt	pinch
1/2	red bell pepper, diced	1/2

Red Curry Paste

Remove and discard the seeds from the chili peppers (if you want a milder paste). Cover with warm water and soak for 30 minutes.

Peel and chop the galanga. Finely slice the lemon grass, discarding the top and root. Roast the coriander and cumin seeds together in a dry skillet over medium heat until a little smoke rises from the seeds (a few minutes). Grind in a mortar and pestle, then add the paprika, turmeric, and cinnamon.

Drain the chilies, saving the liquid. Purée the chilies with all the other ingredients in a blender or processor until a fine paste forms. The texture should be similar to smooth peanut butter. Use the chili water to thin the paste if necessary.

I'm always looking for new ways to serve salmon. It has fast become the most requested dinner item. I love serving salmon with strong flavours because the oil content in the fish stands up so well to bold tastes. Serves 4.

SALMON WITH ROASTED ARTICHOKE,
TOMATO & OLIVE SAUCE

INGREDIENTS

12	roasted artichokes, quartered	12
2	cloves garlic, chopped	2
2 Tbsp.	fresh lemon juice	30 mL
1/3 cup	extra virgin olive oil	75 mL
4	salmon fillets	4
to taste	sea salt and freshly ground black pepper	to taste
4	tomatoes, seeded and cut into 1/4-inch (5-mm) dice	4
1/2 cup	kalamata olives, pitted and slivered	125 mL
1/4 cup	finely chopped fresh parsley or basil	50 mL

METHOD

In a food processor, combine 6 of the artichokes, the garlic, and lemon juice and process until you have a smooth paste. Add the olive oil in a drizzle and process until the sauce is emulsified. It should be thick but liquid enough to sauce a plate. Strain through a sieve into a small saucepan.

Preheat oven to 450°F (230°C).

Place the salmon on a baking sheet lined with aluminum foil. Salt and pepper the salmon and bake for 8 to 10 minutes, depending on thickness, until the salmon flakes easily or reaches your desired degree of doneness. If you prefer, the salmon can also be grilled.

While the salmon is cooking, gently heat the artichoke sauce and add the tomatoes and olives. Place the cooked fillets in the centre of 4 warm dinner plates and spoon sauce around them. Sprinkle the remaining artichoke quarters onto the plates and scatter parsley over all.

To make this you need 4 heatproof plates — the modern-day equivalent of cooking food on hot slabs of rock. The salmon makes a very satisfying sizzle when it hits the plates. Be careful to put the plates on a heatproof surface. Once, during a cooking demonstration of this dish, I welded a plate to a plastic cutting board! Serves 4.

SALMON COOKED ON A PLATE

WITH TOMATO BASIL RELISH

INGREDIENTS

4	medium, ripe tomatoes, seeded and finely diced	4
1 tsp.	salt	5 mL
2 Tbsp.	thinly sliced green onions	30 mL
2 Tbsp.	thinly sliced basil leaves	30 mL
1 Tbsp.	olive oil	15 mL
to taste	salt and pepper	to taste
4	2-oz. (50-g) pieces of salmon fillet, thinly sliced on the diagonal to 1/4-inch (5-mm) thickness	4
	vegetable oil for brushing	

METHOD

Combine the diced tomatoes and 1 tsp. (5 mL) salt. Place in a strainer and allow to drain for 30 minutes. Place the drained tomatoes in a bowl and stir in the onions, basil, and olive oil. Season with salt and pepper.

Preheat oven to 500°F (260°C).

Place 4 heatproof plates in the oven in a single layer for 20 minutes. While the plates are heating, brush the salmon lightly with vegetable oil and season with salt and pepper.

Remove the plates from the oven and immediately place a piece of salmon on each plate. Let the salmon cook for a minute, then spoon the tomato relish on top. Serve immediately, warning your guests that the plates are hot.

We make this for Valentine's Day. When the package is opened at the table, it always elicits delight. Change the hearts to stars for another occasion, such as New Year's Eve. Serves 4.

SALMON BAKED IN PARCHMENT
WITH HEARTS & RIBBONS

INGREDIENTS

2	large carrots, peeled	2
1	radish, peeled	1
1/2	butternut squash, peeled and seeded	1/2
4	16 x 20-inch (40 x 50-cm) pieces of parchment paper	4
4	5 – 6-oz. (150 – 175-g) salmon fillets or steaks	4
to taste	salt and pepper	to taste
2 Tbsp.	coarsely chopped dill	30 mL
2	green onions, julienned	2
1/4 cup	white wine	50 mL
2 Tbsp.	unsalted butter	30 mL
	vegetable oil	

METHOD

To make hearts, cut 1/4 -inch (5-mm) slices from each of the vegetables. Using a small, heart-shaped cookie cutter, cut hearts out of the vegetable slices. To make the ribbons, pare long strips of each of the vegetables with a vegetable peeler.

Fold the parchment paper in half lengthwise. Cut a half-heart shape out of the parchment, starting at the fold. When opened up, you'll have a heart-shaped piece of parchment paper. Stack the vegetable ribbons and cut into a long fine julienne.

Preheat oven to 425°F (220°C).

Season the salmon with salt and pepper. Place a piece on 1 side of each parchment heart.

Toss together the vegetables, dill, and green onions and scatter over the salmon. Add 1 Tbsp. (15 mL) of the white wine and 1/2 Tbsp. (7.5 mL) of the butter to each of the salmon pieces.

This is very easy and always a show-stopper. Serves 4.

SALMON BAKED IN CORN HUSKS
WITH CORN & ZUCCHINI SAUTÉ

INGREDIENTS

4	whole ears of corn	4
4	5 – 6 oz. (150 – 175 g) salmon fillets, skin removed	4
to taste	salt and pepper	to taste
1/4 cup	unsalted butter	50 mL
1 cup	diced red onion	250 mL
1 cup	diced zucchini	250 mL

METHOD

Carefully peel back the corn husks and snap the cob at the bottom, leaving the husks attached to the stem. Discard the silk and any blemished leaves. Set the husks aside.

Cut 2 cups (500 mL) of kernels from the corn and set aside.

Preheat oven to 350°F (180°C).

METHOD — continued

Lightly season the salmon with salt and pepper. Separate the leaves of each corn husk and tuck a salmon fillet into the middle, enclosing it within the husk. Don't try to make it look neat. Tear 4 strips from the discarded leaves and use them to tie the opened end of the husk. Place on a baking sheet and bake for 20 minutes.

While the salmon is baking, melt the butter in a saucepan over medium heat and sauté the red onions until translucent. Sauté the zucchini until it just begins to soften. Add the corn and continue to cook until it's heated through.

Place the salmon on heated plates or a platter. Fold back the top of the corn husks and tuck them under the stem. Spoon the corn sauté over the salmon. Serve immediately.

Wrapping the salmon in sorrel leaves makes it very moist and gives it a lemony flavour. Serves 6 to 8.

BAKED SALMON NOËL

INGREDIENTS

4 – 6-lb.	salmon, cleaned, head removed	2 – 3-kg
1/4 cup	olive oil	50 mL
to taste	freshly ground black pepper	to taste
4 – 6 cups	washed sorrel leaves	1 – 1.5 L
for garnish	sorrel leaves, lemon slices, and sprigs of parsley	for garnish

METHOD

Preheat oven to 350°F (180°C).

Wash the salmon, pat it dry, and lay it on a large piece of aluminum foil. Brush it with oil. Season the interior of the salmon with pepper and stuff with sorrel leaves.

Cover the outside of the salmon with sorrel leaves and wrap tightly in the foil. Put the fish in a baking pan and bake for 1 hour. Test for doneness: when the fish is done, it should flake, but it should also be firm and moist. Depending on its thickness, you may need to bake it for an additional 10 to 15 minutes.

When the fish is cooked, unwrap it, and discard the sorrel leaves. Serve the fish on a warm platter, garnished with sorrel leaves, lemon slices, and sprigs of parsley.

This is best cooked in small portions, so a single serving can be used as an appetizer or two pieces for an entrée. The attractively coloured sauce can be made from freshly prepared beets, although it's a great way to use up leftovers. Salmon portions can be cut from a side of salmon, or ask the fish department of your grocery store to portion it for you. Serves 6.

PAN-ROASTED ROSEMARY SALMON

ON GAMAY BEETROOT BUTTER

INGREDIENTS

12	sprigs fresh rosemary	12
12	3-oz. (75-g) portions of Atlantic salmon fillet, skin on	12
to taste	salt and pepper	to taste
1/4 cup	vegetable oil	50 mL

continues on next page

METHOD

Remove some of the rosemary leaves from the stems by running your fingers against the grain, thus pulling away leaves that can be saved for later use. Stick a rosemary stem through the side of each portion of salmon. Lightly season with salt and pepper.

Heat a heavy-bottomed skillet over medium-high heat and pour in the oil. (Use half the oil if cooking the salmon in 2 batches.) Place the salmon in the skillet skin-side down and cook for 7 to 9 minutes, until it becomes light pink. As it cooks and the rosemary warms, the scent will transfer to the salmon. Loosen the fillets using a spatula. The skin will have become crispy and delicious.

Spoon a little Gamay beetroot butter on the plate and arrange the salmon fillets on top. Sprinkle a little lemon juice over the salmon and enjoy.

Gamay Beetroot Butter

2	beets, cooked in water with a splash of vinegar added, peeled and diced	2
1	shallot, minced	1
1/2 cup	Gamay wine	125 mL
1	lemon, juice of	1
1/2 cup	unsalted butter, cut into pieces and chilled	125 mL
to taste	salt and pepper	to taste

Gamay Beetroot Butter

Place the beets, shallot, wine, and lemon juice in a small saucepan and simmer until the liquid is reduced by three-quarters. Add the butter a piece at a time, stirring constantly, until it's fully incorporated. Season with salt and pepper.

One of the pleasures of this easy recipe is that the salmon tastes good served hot or at room temperature.
Serves 8.

CITRUS-TARRAGON
ROASTED SALMON

INGREDIENTS

1/4 cup	orange juice concentrate	50 mL
1/4 cup	dry sherry	50 mL
2 Tbsp.	fresh tarragon or 1 tsp. (5 mL) dried	30 mL
1 Tbsp.	butter, melted	15 mL
to taste	salt and pepper	to taste
1	clove garlic, minced	1
8	boneless, centre-cut salmon fillets, skin removed, about 3 lb. (1.5 kg)	8

METHOD

Stir the orange juice concentrate with the sherry, tarragon, butter, salt, pepper, and garlic until well combined. Brush all over the fish. Cover and let stand in the refrigerator for 1 hour or up to 4 hours.

Preheat oven to 425°F (220°C).

Place the fish on a buttered baking sheet and brush evenly with the orange mixture in the marinating pan. Place on the centre rack of the oven and cook for 8 to 10 minutes or until the flesh flakes easily with a fork but is still coral-coloured in the centre.

CHILLED SOBA NOODLES WITH SALMON | pages 98 – 99

Karen Barnaby — *The Girls Who Dish: Seconds Anyone?*

FIRST NATIONS-STYLE BAKED COHO SALMON WITH
HONEY & SEAWEED CRUST | pages 130 – 131

Bill Jones

CITRUS SAKE-LACQUERED SALMON | page 133

Aaron Creurer — *Cooks in My Kitchen*

Serves 4

SALMON BAKED IN RED WINE
WITH MUSHROOMS & BACON

INGREDIENTS

1	1½-lb. (750-g) centre-cut salmon fillet, 2 inches (5 cm) thick, skin on	1
to taste	salt and pepper	to taste
¼ cup	finely diced shallots	50 mL
1 cup	dry red wine	250 mL
8 oz.	slab bacon, rind removed, cut into ¼-inch (5-mm) dice	250 g
3 Tbsp.	unsalted butter	45 mL
12 oz.	mushrooms, thickly sliced	375 g
¼ cup	finely chopped fresh parsley	50 mL
1	clove garlic, minced	1

METHOD

Preheat oven to 350°F (180°C).

Place the salmon in a baking dish that holds it snugly. Season with salt and pepper. Scatter the shallots around the salmon and pour the red wine over all. Cover tightly with aluminum foil and bake for 30 minutes. The salmon will still be moist and pink in the middle.

METHOD — continued

While the salmon is baking, slowly render the bacon on medium heat until crisp. Drain the bacon and discard the fat. Set aside.

In a large, non-stick saucepan, melt 1 Tbsp. (15 mL) of the butter over high heat. Add the mushrooms and sauté briskly until lightly browned. Remove from the heat.

Remove the salmon from the oven. Transfer to a plate, cover, and keep warm.

Add the red wine and shallots to the mushrooms. Boil over high heat until the wine is syrupy. Add the bacon and remove from the heat. Whisk in the remaining 2 Tbsp. (30 mL) butter, stirring constantly. Check for seasoning.

Mix together the parsley and garlic. Cut the salmon into 4 pieces and transfer to heated plates. Spoon the sauce over the salmon and sprinkle with the parsley and garlic.

Serves 4

FIRST NATIONS-STYLE BAKED COHO
SALMON WITH HONEY & SEAWEED CRUST

INGREDIENTS

4	6-oz. (175-g) coho (or sockeye) salmon steaks, skin on	4
4	leek strips (or green onion), cut in long, thin lengths	4
to taste	salt and pepper	to taste
1 Tbsp.	honey	15 mL
1/4 cup	dried seaweed, crumbled (bull kelp/kombu or nori)	50 mL
2 Tbsp.	butter	30 mL
1	small onion, peeled and diced	1
1 cup	bread crumbs	250 mL
1 tsp.	minced garlic	5 mL
1	egg	1

continues on next page

METHOD

Preheat oven to 400°F (200°C).

On a cutting board, lay the salmon steaks flat. With a sharp knife, cut out the bones on the inside of the salmon. Be careful not to cut the skin where the bone comes close to the surface. Curl the belly flaps into the middle and make a tight roll of the salmon flesh.

Heat a small saucepan of boiling water and place the leek strips in the water. The strips should be at least 10 inches (25 cm) long. Cook until soft and pliable (about 30 seconds) and transfer to cold water to chill quickly.

Wrap the salmon round with the leek and tie with a knot or bow. Season with salt, pepper, and honey and set aside for at least 10 minutes while you make the topping. Repeat with the remaining steaks.

In a heatproof bowl, add the seaweed and cover with boiling water. Set aside for 5 minutes, then drain. In a non-stick skillet, add the butter and onion and cook

Seaweed Aïoli

2 Tbsp.	dried seaweed, crumbled (bull kelp/kombu or nori)	30 mL
1 Tbsp.	fresh lemon juice (or white wine vinegar)	15 mL
1/4 cup	mayonnaise	50 mL
1	clove garlic, minced	1
to taste	salt, pepper, and hot sauce	to taste

until beginning to brown. Transfer to a bowl and add the bread crumbs, garlic, egg, and seaweed. Stir well to mix. Season with salt and pepper.

Place the salmon steaks in an ovenproof skillet. Divide the seaweed mixture between the steaks and pack onto the top of each. Place in the hot oven and roast for 10 minutes. If the tops aren't browned, finish under a hot broiler. Serve with seaweed aïoli.

Seaweed Aïoli

Place all the ingredients in a blender or food processor and purée until smooth. Season with salt and pepper and refrigerate until needed.

Serves 6

SALMON STEAK

WITH GARLIC & GREEN CHILIES

INGREDIENTS

2 Tbsp.	vegetable oil	30 mL
3 Tbsp.	fresh lemon juice	45 mL
1	medium onion, peeled and chopped	1
1	head of garlic, peeled and chopped	1
1	1-inch (2.5-cm) piece fresh ginger, peeled and chopped	1
2	jalapeño chilies, chopped	2
1/2 tsp.	salt	2 mL
1 tsp.	turmeric	5 mL
6	6-oz. (175-g) salmon steaks	6

METHOD

Using a blender or food processor, combine all the ingredients except the fish. Blend until a fine paste forms. Scrape into a bowl.

Add the salmon steaks and mix well to coat the steaks on both sides. Cover and refrigerate for at least 2 hours.

Heat the barbecue or broiler to high. Place the salmon steaks on the grill or 4 inches (10 cm) away from the broiler element and grill for 3 to 4 minutes on each side, brushing with the marinade.

Serve immediately.

My thought here was to create an Asian-influenced dish that wouldn't overpower the salmon. Make sure that you zest your fruit before you squeeze out the juice. Serves 6.

CITRUS SAKE-LACQUERED SALMON

INGREDIENTS

6	6-oz. (175-g) salmon fillets	6
1/2 cup	honey	125 mL
1 cup	sake	250 mL
2	lemons, grated zest of	2
2	oranges, zest and juice	2
1 Tbsp.	chili paste	15 mL
1 Tbsp.	minced fresh ginger	15 mL

METHOD

Preheat oven to 400°F (200°C).

Place the salmon in a baking dish that will accommodate the fillets in a single layer.

Place all the remaining ingredients in a saucepan and bring to a boil over moderate heat. Cook until it's reduced by half, about 8 minutes. Brush the salmon with the sauce and bake for about 10 minutes, or until the fish starts to feel firm to the touch. To punch up the flavour, brush the salmon with sauce twice during baking.

Change the oven setting to broil and place the fish under the broiler until the honey glaze starts to caramelize. Serve immediately.

Maple syrup, whiskey, and salmon give this rich recipe a taste of Canada. Serve it with small new potatoes and seasonal vegetables. Serves 4.

MAPLE WHISKEY-GLAZED SALMON

INGREDIENTS

4	6-oz. (175-g) salmon fillets or steaks	4
to taste	salt and freshly cracked black pepper	to taste
3 Tbsp.	maple syrup	45 mL
2 Tbsp.	whiskey	30 mL
1 Tbsp.	Dijon mustard	15 mL
1/2	lemon, juice of	1/2
2 tsp.	chopped fresh dill	10 mL
for garnish	dill sprigs and lemon wedges	for garnish

METHOD

Preheat oven to 425°F (220°C).

Place the salmon in a shallow baking dish. Season with salt and pepper. Combine the maple syrup, whiskey, mustard, lemon juice, and chopped dill in a bowl. Mix well and spoon over the fish. Bake for 12 to 15 minutes, or until the fish begins to flake slightly. Divide the salmon among 4 plates and spoon the pan juices over. Garnish with dill sprigs and lemon wedges.

ERIC'S OPTIONS

Feel free to adjust the glaze's level of sweetness or spiciness. For example, if you prefer it less sweet, cut back a little on the maple syrup and add a little extra lemon. If you want it spicy, increase the Dijon mustard. Bourbon can be used instead of whiskey. Trout fillets can replace the salmon.

Any dry rub or spice mixture, like the five-spice powder, is a shortcut to intense, complex flavours. Chinese five-spice powder has a slight licorice flavour and contains equal amounts of ground star anise, Szechuan pepper-corns, cinnamon, cloves, and fennel seed. Serves 4 to 6.

ASIAN-SPICED SALMON
WITH BRAISED BOK CHOY

INGREDIENTS

4	salmon fillets	4
2 Tbsp.	Chinese five-spice powder	30 mL
	olive oil	
4	cloves garlic, chopped	4
1	1-inch (2.5-cm) piece fresh ginger, minced	1
1 cup	chicken stock	250 mL
1 Tbsp.	white miso	15 mL
2	medium bok choy, roughly chopped	2

METHOD

Put the salmon fillets on a cookie sheet and sprinkle the Chinese five-spice powder over them. Let the fillets sit for 30 minutes at room temperature.

Preheat oven to 400°F (200°C).

Place the fillets in the oven and bake to desired doneness. I prefer to cook salmon for 7 to 8 minutes per inch (2.5 cm), which leaves the salmon moist, with a little line of pink on the inside.

Add enough olive oil to a skillet to thinly cover the bottom. Place the skillet over high heat, add the garlic and ginger, and sauté. Add the stock, miso, and bok choy and cook until the bok choy is slightly softened but not overcooked.

To serve, put a generous helping of the broth in each shallow bowl, distributing the bok choy evenly. Place the salmon on top.

POACHED & STEAMED

Salmon looks stunning surrounded by this black bean vinaigrette, and it can be served cold in the summer.
Also try the vinaigrette with poached or grilled prawns for an exceptional combination. Serves 4.

POACHED SALMON

WITH GINGER & BLACK BEAN VINAIGRETTE

INGREDIENTS

1 cup	white wine	250 mL
4	1/4-inch (5-mm) slices fresh ginger, lightly crushed	4
1	star anise	1
1 Tbsp.	sugar	15 mL
2	green onions, lightly crushed	2
2 tsp.	salt	10 mL
1	whole dried chili pepper	1
4 cups	water	1 L
4	6-oz. (175-g) salmon fillets	4

continues on next page

METHOD

Combine all the ingredients except the salmon in a non-corrodible saucepan that will hold the salmon snugly. Bring to a boil, then simmer for 15 minutes, partially covered with a lid. Slip the salmon fillets into the liquid and poach gently for 10 minutes. Remove from the liquid.

If you wish to serve the salmon cold, cool to room temperature, then cover and refrigerate. (The salmon may be prepared 1 day in advance.) To serve hot, transfer to heated plates or a platter. Spoon the vinaigrette around the salmon and serve immediately.

Ginger & Black Bean Vinaigrette

2	medium cloves garlic, minced	2
1 Tbsp.	minced fresh ginger	15 mL
1/2 cup	pickled ginger	125 mL
3 Tbsp.	pickled ginger juice	45 mL
2 Tbsp.	apple cider vinegar	30 mL
3/4 tsp.	salt	4 mL
3 Tbsp.	sugar	45 mL
1/4 cup	fermented black beans*	50 mL
3/4 cup	vegetable oil	175 mL

* Available at oriental markets and well-stocked supermarkets.

Ginger & Black Bean Vinaigrette

Make the vinaigrette at least 1 day before using.

Combine all the ingredients except the vegetable oil in a food processor or blender. Pulse until very finely chopped. With the motor running, add the vegetable oil in a slow steady stream and process until well blended. Cover and refrigerate. The vinaigrette will keep for up to 1 week in the refrigerator. Bring it to room temperature before serving.

In classical French cooking, ballotines are chicken legs that have been boned, stuffed, and roasted. This dish contains no chicken and no legs, and it isn't roasted, but it's a fine dish featuring salmon rolled in cabbage leaves and then poached. The delicate flavour of the herbs and the mild cabbage pair well with the salmon. This is fine served warm or cold, so make it in advance for a special occasion. Serves 10 to 12.

SALMON & CABBAGE BALLOTINE

INGREDIENTS

1	onion, finely sliced	1
1	bulb garlic, split horizontally	1
1	stalk celery, finely sliced	1
1	carrot, finely sliced	1
1	leek, chopped	1
1	bay leaf	1
1 tsp.	black peppercorns	5 mL
6	twigs fresh thyme	6
1 Tbsp.	minced fresh ginger	15 mL
2	lemons, zest and juice of	2
8 cups	water	2 L
1	Savoy or napa cabbage	1
1	onion, minced	1
1	stalk celery, minced	1
1 tsp.	olive oil	5 mL
1	2-lb. (1-kg) boneless salmon fillet, skin removed	1

continues on next page

METHOD

Place the onion, garlic, celery, carrot, and leek in a large heavy ovenproof dish, then add the bay leaf, peppercorns, thyme, ginger, zest and juice of 1 lemon, and water. Bring to a boil and simmer for 30 minutes to extract the flavours and reduce it slightly.

While the poaching liquid is simmering, pull about 12 leaves from the outside of the head of cabbage. Immerse each leaf into the simmering liquid, cooking it just long enough to soften the fibres and make the leaf pliable. Remove the leaves and cool under cold water. Trim out the thick stem from the centre of each leaf.

Sauté the minced onion and celery in the olive oil, adding small amounts of water as needed to prevent browning. Place half the sautéed vegetables in a food processor with half the salmon and purée. Add the fresh herbs, green onions, the egg if using one, the remaining lemon juice and the zest, salt, and hot chili

2 tsp.	minced fresh thyme	10 mL
1 tsp.	minced fresh dillweed	5 mL
2 tsp.	minced fresh lemon balm	10 mL
2	green onions, minced	2
1	egg (optional)	1
1 Tbsp.	whipping cream (optional)	15 mL
to taste	salt and hot chili flakes	to taste

flakes. Add the cream if you wish at the very end, being careful not to overprocess the mixture. Slice the remaining salmon into 1/2-inch (1-cm) strips up to 10 inches (25 cm) long, then assemble a bed of overlapping cabbage leaves on a clean kitchen towel, using all the blanched and trimmed leaves. The bed should be 2 layers deep and about 12 inches (30 cm) long and 8 inches (20 cm) wide. Starting and ending with the salmon strips, build layers of salmon strips, sautéed vegetables, and purée in the middle of the cabbage leaves, leaving 3 to 4 inches (8 to 10 cm) on all sides. Roll it up jelly-roll fashion, encasing the whole in the kitchen towel. Tie the ends with butcher's twine and then tie the cylinder at intervals.

Gently place the wrapped cylinder in the hot poaching liquid, cover, and bring to a boil. Reduce the heat to a simmer and cook for about an hour. On a cutting board, carefully unwrap the cylinder and check for doneness. If cooked through, allow to cool for 10 to 20 minutes before slicing into rounds about 1/2 inch (1 cm) thick.

The key to perfect poached salmon is to simmer it very gently until it's just cooked. If you let it boil, the fish will become dry and fall apart. Serves 4.

SALMON POACHED IN SAFFRON
BROTH WITH CRANBERRY CURRY BUTTER

INGREDIENTS

12	nugget potatoes	12
2 Tbsp.	butter	30 mL
1/4 cup	chopped onion	50 mL
1/4 cup	chopped leek, white part only	50 mL
1/2 cup	dry white wine	125 mL
1 tsp.	saffron	5 mL
8 cups	Salmon Stock (page 22)	2 L
1 Tbsp.	fresh lemon juice	15 mL
4	7-oz. (200-g) salmon fillets	4
1/2 cup	mixed julienne vegetables (red and green bell peppers, celery, carrot, and red onion)	125 mL

continues on next page

METHOD

Place the potatoes in a small saucepan and cover with cold salted water. Bring to a boil and cook until tender, about 40 minutes. Keep warm until ready to use.

Melt the butter in a large saucepan over medium heat. Add the onion and leek and sweat for 5 minutes, or until soft. Do not brown. Add the wine and cook until the liquid is reduced by three-quarters. Add the saffron, salmon stock, and lemon juice. Bring to a boil. Reduce the heat and gently simmer for 30 minutes.

Strain the stock, discard the onion and leek, then return the stock to the heat. Immerse the salmon in the stock and poach gently for 8 minutes. Add the julienne vegetables and cook for 2 minutes.

To serve, place 3 warm potatoes in each bowl. Top with a salmon fillet. Spoon a little saffron stock and vegetables on top. Place a slice of cranberry curry butter on top of each piece of salmon.

Serve immediately.

Cranberry Curry Butter
Makes 1½ cups (375 mL)

½ cup	dried cranberries	125 mL
8 oz.	butter	250 g
1½ tsp.	ground cumin	7 mL
1½ tsp.	ground turmeric	7 mL
1½ tsp.	ground coriander	7 mL
1 tsp.	ground cayenne pepper	5 mL
1 tsp.	minced garlic	5 mL
1 tsp.	fresh lemon juice	5 mL

Cranberry Curry Butter

Rehydrate the cranberries in very hot water for 10 minutes. Drain and pat them dry with a paper towel. In a food processor, combine all the ingredients except the cranberries and pulse to combine well. Transfer to a small bowl and fold in the cranberries. Lay out 2 sheets of plastic wrap about 18 inches (45 cm) long, 1 on top of the other. Place the butter on the plastic in a log shape and roll it up.

Twist the ends of the roll and tie tightly with string. Chill for at least 2 hours before using. Freeze leftovers for future use.

Drinking a Cinzano one summer evening, I caught the scent of grilling salmon wafting its way through the neighbourhood. A sip, a sniff, another sip, and an idea was born. Salmon is deceptively rich and it pairs rather unlikely ingredients with great success. The red vermouth is sweet Cinzano, which plays off well against the earthy flavours of smoked bacon and mild Savoy cabbage. *Serves 4.*

SALMON

WITH BACON, VERMOUTH & CABBAGE

INGREDIENTS

2 slices	side bacon, finely sliced	2 slices
1	medium onion, finely sliced	1
4	cloves garlic, minced	4
1/4	head Savoy or napa cabbage, finely shredded	1/4
1	lemon, juice and zest of	1
2 tsp.	minced fresh thyme	10 mL
1/2 cup	sweet red Cinzano	125 mL
4	5-oz. (150-g) salmon fillets	4
to taste	salt and pepper	to taste

NOTE

Using smoky or high-fat foods as flavour agents rather than main ingredients is a sensible way to use less for more. The bacon in this dish adds its unmistakable flavour and aroma, but 2 slim slices add a minimal amount of fat. If you wish, substitute prosciutto or pancetta.

METHOD

In a non-stick skillet, cook the bacon until it releases its fat and begins to colour. Discard the fat, then add the onion and garlic. Cook until tender and transparent, about 5 minutes, adding small amounts of water as needed to prevent burning or colouring.

Add the cabbage, lemon juice and zest, and cook the cabbage until it loses its bulk and softens, about 5 minutes. Add the thyme and Cinzano. Bring to a boil, reduce the liquid by half, and then add the salmon fillets, rearranging the vegetables in the skillet to cover the fish. Cover and reduce the heat to low. Steam the fish for about 7 minutes or until just done. Add salt and pepper to taste.

This aromatic dish is excellent as the centrepiece of a multi-course Asian dinner or served alone with rice for a delicious, low-fat weeknight meal. Serves 6.

BLACK BEAN-GINGER
POACHED SALMON

INGREDIENTS

2¹/₂ cups	water	625 mL
2¹/₂ cups	Salmon Stock (see page 22) or chicken broth or clam juice	625 mL
¹/₂ cup	sake (or medium sherry)	125 mL
¹/₄ cup	fermented black beans, rinsed	50 mL
¹/₃ cup	tamari	75 mL
3 Tbsp.	hoisin sauce	45 mL
2 Tbsp.	mirin	30 mL
1 Tbsp.	brown sugar	15 mL
1 Tbsp.	freshly grated ginger	15 mL
¹/₂ tsp.	hot sauce	2 mL
2	cloves garlic, minced	2
6	6-oz. (175-g) salmon fillets, skin removed	6
¹/₂ cup	julienned daikon or radish	125 mL
6 – 8	chives	6 – 8

METHOD

Bring the water, broth, sake, black beans, tamari, hoisin, mirin, brown sugar, ginger, hot sauce, and garlic to a boil in a fish poacher or Dutch oven set over high heat. Reduce the heat and simmer for 10 minutes. Reduce the heat until the liquid is barely simmering.

Use a large, flat metal spatula or palette knife to place as many fillets as will fit into the pan without crowding. Place a lid just smaller than the pan's circumference on top of the fish to keep it submerged. Poach for 7 to 9 minutes or until the fish is opaque on the outside but still coral-coloured in the middle. Slide the spatula lengthwise under each piece of fish and place in wide individual Japanese-style soup plates or pasta bowls. Cover and set aside. Repeat until all the fillets are cooked.

Increase the heat to high and bring the poaching liquid to a boil. Add the daikon and cook for 1 minute. Ladle a little poaching liquid over each piece of fish. Chop the chives into ³/4 -inch (2-cm) lengths and sprinkle into the bowls.

Poaching salmon doesn't have to be a difficult process. By using an instant-read thermometer, available at most kitchen stores, you can immediately tell when the salmon is done. This prevents overcooking your portions of fish to the point that they crumble as you remove them from the poaching liquid. *Serves 6.*

POACHED SALMON
ON SWEET PEPPER SAUCES

INGREDIENTS

4 cups	Salmon Stock (page 22)	1 L
1 cup	white wine	250 mL
2	lemons, sliced	2
2	sprigs fresh thyme	2
to taste	salt and pepper	to taste
6	6-oz. (175-g) salmon fillets, pinbones removed	6

Sweet Pepper Sauces

2	red bell peppers, seeded	2
2	yellow bell peppers, seeded	2
1	small Yukon Gold potato, peeled and diced	1
1	onion, diced	1
2	cloves garlic, sliced	2
1 cup	white wine	250 mL
1 cup	water	250 mL
2	sprigs fresh thyme	2
to taste	salt and pepper	to taste

METHOD

Preheat oven to 275°F (140°C).

In a flat-bottomed roasting pan or saucepan with sides at least 4 inches (10 cm) high, simmer stock, wine, lemons, thyme, salt, and pepper. Place salmon pieces in the liquid, leaving some space between them for even cooking, and remove pan from heat.

Cover pan with its lid or foil and place it in the oven. Cook for 15 to 20 minutes, checking temperature after 15 minutes. The internal temperature of the salmon should be 145°F (62°C) and the flesh should feel firm. Remember, the salmon will continue to cook after it's removed from the oven. Using a slotted spoon or spatula, gently remove each piece from the liquid, and place on paper towels or a rack to drain. Chill for at least 4 hours before serving.

To prepare sauces, place red and yellow peppers in separate small saucepans (or sauces can be made one at a time) with half of each of the remaining ingredients. Simmer for 20 minutes. Remove sprigs of thyme and purée each sauce separately with a hand blender or in a food processor. Strain, season to taste, and chill.

To serve, spoon each sauce onto the plate for a side-by-side contrast, or create your own pattern with dots and lines. Place a salmon piece on each plate.

The best part of planning to serve a chilled dish is that most of the work can be done ahead of time so that before serving all you have to do is assemble. If you like salmon rare, remove it sooner than 20 minutes. If you want your salmon fully cooked, then leave it for the full cooking time. Eat food that makes you happy.

Serves 4

VIETNAMESE-STYLE STEAMED CHUM
SALMON & TORTILLA ROLLS

INGREDIENTS

6 oz.	chum salmon, cut in strips	175 g
1 cup	leftover cooked rice	250 mL
1	small carrot, peeled and shredded	1
1/2 cup	shiitake (or button) mushrooms, stemmed and diced	125 mL
1/2 cup	bean sprouts	125 mL
1	green onion, sliced	1
to taste	salt and pepper	to taste
2 Tbsp.	hoisin sauce	30 mL
1 tsp.	hot sauce	5 mL
1 tsp.	sesame oil	5 mL
1	garlic clove, minced	1
1 Tbsp.	finely chopped mint	15 mL
1 Tbsp.	finely chopped basil	15 mL
4	large white tortillas	4
2 – 3	cabbage leaves	2 – 3

METHOD

In a mixing bowl, combine the salmon, cold rice, carrot, mushrooms, bean sprouts, and green onion. Season well with salt and pepper and set aside until needed.

In a small bowl, combine the hoisin, hot sauce, sesame oil, garlic, mint, and basil. Mix well and set aside. In a large saucepan or wok, add 2 cups (500 mL) water and place a steaming tray on top. Place the cabbage leaves on the base of the steaming tray, cover with a lid, and bring to a boil.

On a flat surface, lay out a tortilla and cover its surface completely with the hoisin mixture. Add one-quarter of the salmon mixture in a row along the side closest to you. Fold the tortilla over the filling, away from you, and roll into a compact cylinder. Cut the log in half and set aside, seam-side down. Repeat with the remaining tortillas and filling. Place the rolls on the cabbage leaves in the hot steamer. Cook for 7 to 8 minutes. Serve warm.

Serve this rich dish with basmati rice and your favourite chutney. For a slightly richer sauce, stir in coconut milk in place of some or all of the stock. For a vegetarian dish that hits all the right notes, make it without the fish. Leftovers make a great rice or pasta sauce, and a divine soup. Serves 4.

PAN-STEAMED SALMON

WITH CURRIED SPINACH & CHICKPEAS

INGREDIENTS

4	5-oz. (150-g) salmon fillets	4
2¹/2 tsp.	curry powder	12 mL
1 Tbsp.	canola oil	15 mL
1	onion, minced	1
2	carrots, grated	2
4	cloves garlic, minced	4
1 Tbsp.	grated fresh ginger	15 mL
1 Tbsp.	canola oil	15 mL
1 cup	cooked chickpeas	250 mL
1 cup	chicken or vegetable stock	250 mL
1 – 2 tsp.	cornstarch dissolved in cold water	5 – 10 mL
1 bunch	spinach, well washed	1
1 Tbsp.	honey	15 mL
1	lemon, zest and juice of	1
to taste	salt and hot chili flakes	to taste
2 Tbsp.	minced cilantro	30 mL

METHOD

Sprinkle the salmon with 1 tsp. (5 mL) of the curry powder. Pan-steam the salmon in the oil over low heat in a non-stick skillet. Use a lid that fits snugly over the fish and turn the fish several times. Reduce the heat if the fish sizzles or browns. After 7 to 10 minutes, remove the fish to a plate and cover loosely to keep warm.

Cook the onion, carrots, garlic, and ginger in the same skillet with the remaining oil until the vegetables are tender, about 5 to 7 minutes. Stir in the remaining 1¹/2 tsp. (7 mL) of curry powder. Add the chickpeas and the stock. Bring to a boil and thicken with the cornstarch dissolved in cold water. Add the spinach when the sauce is translucent and cook until just wilted. Add the honey and lemon. Adjust the seasoning with salt and hot chili flakes.

Arrange on a deep platter and top with the salmon. Sprinkle with cilantro and serve hot.

Serves 6

SKATE & SALMON PAUPIETTES
IN LEMON & PARSLEY SAUCE

INGREDIENTS

8 oz.	fresh salmon fillet	250 g
2	ice cubes	2
1	egg yolk	1
1 tsp.	pastis (or sambuca)	5 mL
1/4 cup	butter, softened to room temperature	50 mL
2 Tbsp.	whipping cream	30 mL
to taste	salt	to taste
2 lb.	fresh skate wings	1 kg
1 cup	dry Riesling or Sauvignon Blanc wine	250 mL
1 Tbsp.	peeled shallot, cut into brunoise	15 mL
1 Tbsp.	fresh lemon juice	15 mL
2 Tbsp.	chopped parsley	30 mL
12	small potatoes, cooked and peeled	12

METHOD

Cut the salmon fillet into bite-size pieces. Purée the pieces in a food processor with the ice cubes. While the motor is running, add the egg yolk and pastis. Add 1 Tbsp. (15 mL) of the butter slowly, then add the cream in a slow, steady stream. Season the mousse with salt. Set aside.

Lay out the skate wings flesh-side down. Place the salmon mousse at 1 end of each fillet. Roll the fillet up so that the mousse is contained inside it. Wrap this paupiette with plastic film and twist the ends of the film to maintain a cylindrical shape. Repeat until all the paupiettes are rolled and wrapped. Steam the paupiettes in a vegetable steamer, covered, for 10 minutes. They are ready when the interior temperature reaches 150°F (65°C). Set aside.

Pour the wine into a saucepan over medium heat. Add the shallot brunoise. Boil down to a syrupy consistency. Add the lemon juice and boil for 30 seconds. Add the parsley and whisk in the remaining 3 Tbsp. (45 mL) of butter.

To serve, warm 6 plates. Remove the plastic film from the paupiettes. Slice the paupiettes carefully with a sharp carving knife. Arrange 3 slices in an overlapping pattern on each plate and nap with the sauce. Place 2 potatoes on each plate. Serve immediately.

SAUTÉ & STIRFRY

Serve this salmon with rice cooked in chicken broth and orange juice (half and half) instead of water. Serves 4.

SALMON FILLETS
WITH CITRUS BEURRE BLANC

INGREDIENTS		
1/2	grapefruit	1/2
1/2 cup	dry white wine	125 mL
1/2 cup	white wine vinegar	125 mL
1 Tbsp.	finely chopped onion	15 mL
1 Tbsp.	heavy cream	15 mL
1 cup	butter, softened	250 mL
1 Tbsp.	finely chopped fresh lemon balm leaves	15 mL
2 Tbsp.	olive oil	30 mL
4	6 – 7 oz. (175 – 200 g) salmon fillets	4
to taste	salt and freshly ground pepper	to taste

METHOD

Remove the pulp from the grapefruit, working over a small bowl to catch the juice. Discard the seeds. Purée the pulp in a blender or food processor.

In a small saucepan, combine the wine, vinegar, and onion, and bring to a boil over medium heat. Reduce the heat to low and simmer gently until the mixture is syrupy and the liquid is almost evaporated. Whisk in the cream. Whisk in the butter, 1/2 cup (125 mL) at a time. Don't allow the mixture to boil. Stir in the grapefruit purée and lemon balm. Keep warm.

In a large heavy skillet, heat the olive oil over medium-high heat until very hot.

Season the salmon with salt and pepper. Place the salmon in the skillet and cook for 3 to 5 minutes on each side or until the salmon is opaque and flakes easily when tested with the tip of a sharp knife.

Transfer the salmon to warmed serving plates and pour the sauce over it.

Just remember, looks don't count first with cooks, and it's a good thing. Once, to my chagrin, this dish was seriously considered for The Ugliest Dish of the Year Award by a group of professional eaters. It didn't win and they did enjoy eating it. This dish works equally well if you substitute barbecued duck for the salmon. Serves 6.

BRAISED MUSHROOMS
WITH SLIVERED BARBECUED SALMON

INGREDIENTS

16	dried Chinese black mushrooms	16
1 Tbsp.	canola oil	15 mL
1	Asian eggplant, cut into ½-inch (1-cm) dice	1
2 Tbsp.	puréed fresh ginger	30 mL
2 Tbsp.	puréed garlic	30 mL
2 – 4 cups	chicken stock, vegetable stock, or water	500 mL – 1 L
1 bunch	green onions, cut into 3-inch (8-cm) lengths	1 bunch
¼ cup	dark or mushroom soy sauce	50 mL
1 Tbsp.	honey	15 mL
8 oz.	hot-smoked salmon, broken into chunks	250 g
1 tsp.	sesame oil	5 mL
½ tsp.	hot chili flakes	2 mL
for garnish	sesame seeds, cilantro sprigs	for garnish

METHOD

Soak the mushrooms in hot water until soft and pliable. Discard the stems, strain, and reserve the soaking water. Heat the oil in a non-stick skillet and stir in the eggplant, ginger, and garlic. Start adding stock or water, including the mushroom-soaking water. (The eggplant, greedy little sponges, will soak up lots of liquid, so add enough that the dish always looks juicy.) Stir in the green onions and mushroom caps, then the dark or mushroom soy sauce and honey. Simmer for about 20 minutes or until the eggplant and mushroom caps are tender.

Add the chunks of hot-smoked salmon, sesame oil, and hot chili flakes and heat until warmed through. Serve over rice or noodles. Sprinkle with sesame seeds and garnish with sprigs of cilantro.

I like to serve this salmon with a large mound of buttery mashed potatoes. It's a great combination and a staff favourite at the restaurant. Serves 4.

SALMON WITH SAUTÉED
VEGETABLES & BALSAMIC BUTTER SAUCE

INGREDIENTS

1 cup	balsamic vinegar	250 mL
2 Tbsp.	olive oil	30 mL
4	6-oz. (175-g) salmon fillets	4
to taste	salt and freshly ground black pepper	to taste
3 Tbsp.	unsalted butter	45 mL
1 cup	leeks, white part only, cut on a diagonal	250 mL
1½ cups	sliced mixed mushrooms	375 mL
2 Tbsp.	white wine	30 mL
8 oz.	fresh spinach leaves, stems removed	250 g

continues on next page

METHOD

In a small saucepan reduce the vinegar over medium-high heat until it reaches a syrupy consistency. It will reduce to about 2 Tbsp. (30 mL) and will take about 15 minutes. Set aside.

Preheat oven to 450°F (230°C).

Heat the olive oil in a large ovenproof skillet over medium heat. Season the salmon fillets with salt and pepper. When the oil is hot, place the salmon fillets in the skillet, flesh-side down. Sear for 1 to 2 minutes, depending on the thickness of the fillets. Turn the salmon skin-side down, place the skillet in the hot oven, and cook for 4 to 5 minutes.

Heat the butter in a large skillet. When the butter is hot, add the leeks and sauté over medium-high heat until they begin to soften. Add the mushrooms and continue to sauté for 2 to 3 minutes. Deglaze the pan with the white wine and season with salt and pepper. Add

Butter Sauce
Makes about 3/4 cup (175 mL)

1 Tbsp.	butter	15 mL
2	shallots, thinly sliced	2
1 cup	dry white wine	250 mL
1 tsp.	fresh lemon juice	5 mL
2 Tbsp.	whipping cream	30 mL
1/2 cup	diced cold butter	125 mL
to taste	salt and white pepper	to taste

the spinach and cook for 1 minute or until the spinach has barely wilted. Remove from the heat.

To serve, place equal amounts of the mushroom mixture on each of 4 dinner plates. Place the cooked salmon on top of the mushrooms. Pour the butter sauce on top of the salmon and a little on the plate. To finish, drizzle a little of the balsamic reduction over the salmon and the butter sauce.

Butter Sauce

Melt the 1 Tbsp. (15 mL) butter in a small saucepan over low heat. Add the shallots and sauté gently until transparent. Add the white wine and lemon juice and cook until almost all the liquid has evaporated. Add the cream and heat. Remove the pan from the heat, add the diced butter, and whisk until smooth. Adjust seasoning with salt and pepper. Strain. For a creamier sauce, blend it in the blender on high speed for 30 to 60 seconds.

I love salmon and fennel, particularly in this recipe where they're combined with the sweetness of the sherry, the sweet-tart freshness of the oranges, and the heat of the peppers. It's also a dish that comes together quickly, even more so when you use canned roasted peppers. Serves 6.

FENNEL-CRUSTED SALMON
WITH BLOOD ORANGE & ROASTED RED PEPPER VINAIGRETTE

INGREDIENTS

1¹/₂ Tbsp.	crushed fennel seed	22 mL
1 tsp.	crushed white peppercorns	5 mL
1 tsp.	kosher salt	5 mL
4	salmon fillets, each about 2 inches (5 cm) thick	4
for frying	olive oil	for frying
4 cups	arugula	1 L

continues on next page

METHOD

Preheat oven to 400°F (200°C).

Mix together the fennel seed, peppercorns, and salt. Rub the salmon fillets with olive oil and coat with the spice mixture. In an ovenproof skillet over medium-high heat, heat a thin layer of olive oil. Add the salmon, skin-side up, and fry for 4 to 5 minutes. Turn the salmon over and finish in the oven for another 3 to 5 minutes (depending on thickness), until cooked to the desired texture.

To serve, place a mound of arugula on each plate, top with the salmon, and drizzle with the vinaigrette.

Blood Orange & Roasted Pepper Vinaigrette

Makes 1½ cups (375 mL)

2	red bell peppers	2
1	shallot, minced	1
⅔ cup	fresh blood orange juice	150 mL
1 tsp.	crushed fennel seed	5 mL
2 Tbsp.	sherry vinegar	15 mL
½ cup	extra virgin olive oil	125 mL
2 Tbsp.	hazelnut oil	30 mL
to taste	kosher salt and pepper	to taste

Blood Orange & Roasted Pepper Vinaigrette

To roast the peppers, place them directly under the broiler. As the flesh blackens, turn the peppers until they are black all over. Remove from the oven, place in a bowl, and cover with plastic wrap or a plate for about 5 minutes. When cool enough to handle, remove the blackened skin, pull out the stem and seeds, and rinse. Finely chop the peppers.

Whisk the peppers, shallot, juice, fennel seed, and vinegar in a mixing bowl. Slowly add the oils, whisking to emulsify. Season with salt and pepper.

Everyone is looking for an innovative way to serve salmon. This Asian-flavoured dish is rich in taste but not in calories. You can serve it to family or at your most elegant dinner party. Try it with wasabi mashed potatoes for a real taste treat. Serves 8.

SEARED SALMON FILLET WITH
SCALLIONS, PORTOBELLO MUSHROOMS & DARK GINGER SAUCE

INGREDIENTS

2 bunches	green onions	2 bunches
10 oz.	portobello mushrooms, sliced	300 g
3/4 cup	peanut oil	175 mL
2 Tbsp.	sesame seeds	30 mL
2 tsp.	sesame oil	10 mL
1	2-inch (5-cm) piece fresh ginger, peeled and cut in julienne strips	1
2 Tbsp.	water	30 mL
1/3 cup	soy sauce	75 mL
1 tsp.	cornstarch	5 mL
1/4 cup	brown sugar	50 mL
1/2 tsp.	freshly ground black pepper	2 mL
3 lb.	salmon fillets, skin removed, cut into 8 pieces	1.5 kg
1/4 cup	water	50 mL

METHOD

Clean the green onions, discarding all but 3 inches (8 cm) of the greens. Cut into 1 1/2-inch (4-cm) pieces on a 45-degree angle. Sauté the mushrooms in 2 Tbsp. (30 mL) of the peanut oil. Set aside.

Toast the sesame seeds in a dry, clean skillet over medium heat until brown. Remove to a small bowl.

Heat another 2 Tbsp. (30 mL) of the peanut oil and the sesame oil in the same skillet and add the ginger. Add the green onions and stir-fry for 30 seconds or until tender. Add the water, 4 tsp. (20 mL) of the soy sauce and cornstarch, and cook until the sauce has thickened. Add the cooked mushrooms.

Mix the sugar and pepper in a large bowl. Dip 1 side of each salmon fillet into the mixture and place on a platter. Heat the remaining 1/2 cup (125 mL) of the peanut oil in a large, non-stick skillet over medium-high

ASIAN-SPICED SALMON WITH BRAISED BOK CHOY | page 135

Gail Norton — *Double Dishing*

FENNEL-CRUSTED SALMON WITH BLOOD ORANGE & ROASTED
RED PEPPER VINAIGRETTE | pages 158 – 159

Pam Fortier — *Cooks in My Kitchen*

heat. Add the salmon and cook for about 3 minutes, until the bottom is browned and caramelized. Pour the remaining ¼ cup (50 mL) soy sauce and the water into the skillet. Cover and continue cooking for about 3 to 5 minutes, until the fish is glazed and just opaque throughout. The salmon can be cooked in batches, but drain the skillet and add more peanut oil, soy sauce, and water between batches.

To serve, warm the green onion and mushroom mixture by stirring over medium-high heat. Transfer the salmon to individual plates. Spoon the onions and mushrooms over the salmon and sprinkle with the toasted sesame seeds. Serve immediately.

Rubs are perfect for seafood. They impart flavour instantly and, unlike acidic marinades, they don't draw the natural juices from the fish. Serve with oven fries or corn on the cob and grilled asparagus. Make your own rubs using spices found in curries or Middle Eastern dishes, adding yogurt or honey. Serves 4.

SALMON WITH SWEET SPICE RUB
& ROASTED TOMATO SALSA

INGREDIENTS

1 tsp.	cumin seed	5 mL
1 tsp.	coriander seed	5 mL
1 tsp.	chili powder	5 mL
1/2 tsp.	ground cinnamon	2 mL
1/4 tsp.	freshly ground black pepper	1 mL
2 Tbsp.	dark brown sugar	30 mL
4	6-oz. (175-g) salmon fillets (with or without skin)	4
1/4 cup	olive oil	60 mL
to taste	coarse sea salt and freshly ground black pepper	to taste
1/2 cup	finely diced onion	125 mL
1/2 cup	finely diced sun-dried tomatoes (oil-packed or rehydrated)	125 mL
6	Roma tomatoes, cut in half lengthwise	6
1	bulb roasted garlic	1
to taste	coarse sea salt and freshly ground black pepper	to taste
2 Tbsp.	unsalted butter or olive oil	30 mL

METHOD

Preheat oven to 350°F (180°C).

Place the cumin and coriander in a small skillet, and dry-roast them over medium-high heat until they're warm and fragrant — a few may even pop. Once roasted, grind them in a mortar and pestle or coffee grinder. Combine the toasted spices with the chili powder, cinnamon, pepper, and sugar.

Prepare the salmon by rubbing all sides with 2 Tbsp. (30 mL) of the olive oil. Coat the top of the salmon evenly with the spice mixture. If the pieces are thick, leaving the sides uncoated for contrasting colour is a nice touch. Let the salmon rest for 30 minutes or prepare it in advance and refrigerate. Just before cooking, sprinkle it with salt and pepper.

Sauté the onion in the remaining 2 Tbsp. (30 mL) olive oil until softened. Choose a small ovenproof skillet for this step — one that can hold the tomatoes in a single layer. Once the onions are soft, place the sun-dried tomatoes on the onions and arrange the Roma tomatoes, cut-side down, on top. Place the skillet in the oven. After about 12 to 15 minutes, check the tomatoes. If the skins are wrinkled you can slip them off. When the tomato skins are removed, mix together all the skillet ingredients. Squeeze the roasted garlic cloves from their skins into the mixture. Season with salt and pepper. Set aside and keep warm.

Raise the oven temperature to 400°F (200°C). Heat the butter or oil, preferably in a non-stick skillet, until very hot. Sear the spice-rubbed side of the salmon just long enough to set the spices and create a crust. Gently turn the salmon over and transfer the skillet to the oven to finish cooking. Depending on the thickness, it will be done in 4 to 6 minutes. It should be firm to the touch, springy, not soft, but definitely not hard and flaking! Serve with the warm tomato salsa.

This isn't a traditional dish, but I think a Thai person would like the traditional approach of using different textures in one dish. The rice paper becomes crisp when fried, and the salmon inside is soft and moist. The sauce has a creamy texture and ties together all the flavours. I sometimes use this as an appetizer, serving 1 package per person. Serves 4.

SALMON IN RICE PAPER WRAPS
WITH COCONUT GINGER SAUCE

INGREDIENTS

8	salmon fillets, about 1 inch (2.5 cm) thick, 4 inches (10 cm) long, 2 inches (5 cm) wide	8
8 tsp.	soy sauce	40 mL
8	round rice paper wrappers, 8 inches (20 cm) in diameter	8
16	basil leaves	16
8 tsp.	chopped fresh ginger	40 mL
2 Tbsp.	peanut or vegetable oil	30 mL

continues on next page

METHOD

Season each piece of salmon with 1 tsp. (5 mL) of soy sauce. Set aside.

Fill a wide shallow pan with warm water and spread a dish towel on a counter. Dip 1 rice paper wrapper in the water for about 10 seconds to soften it, then place on the towel.

Place 2 basil leaves in the centre of the rice paper. Place a piece of salmon on top of the basil. Place 1 tsp. (5 mL) of ginger on top of the salmon. Fold the wrap around the salmon to enclose it securely. Repeat with the remaining ingredients. Place the salmon packages seam-side down on a plate in a single layer. Cover and refrigerate until cooking time. It can be prepared to this point up to 4 hours ahead.

At cooking time, heat the oil in a well-seasoned or non-stick skillet over high heat and place the salmon packages seam-side down in the skillet. Cook uncovered for 2 minutes. Turn over and cook for an additional

Coconut Ginger Sauce
Makes about 1½ cups (375 mL)

This sauce has a creamy texture and a subtle flavour. It's ideal with salmon but wonderful with any seafood.

1 Tbsp.	vegetable oil	15 mL
2 tsp.	chopped shallots	10 mL
2 tsp.	chopped fresh ginger	10 mL
1 cup	coconut milk	250 mL
2 Tbsp.	soy sauce	30 mL
2 Tbsp.	palm or brown sugar	30 mL
1 Tbsp.	lime juice	15 mL
1 tsp.	lime zest	5 mL
2 Tbsp.	chopped basil	30 mL

2 minutes. Remove the skillet from the heat, cover, and set aside for 3 or 4 minutes while you make the sauce.

Place one-quarter of the sauce on each of 4 plates. Place the wraps seam-side down so the basil leaves show through the rice paper.

Coconut Ginger Sauce

Heat the oil in a saucepan over high heat. Add the shallot and ginger and fry until they are soft and translucent. Add the coconut milk. Bring it almost to a boil and add the soy sauce, sugar, lime juice, zest, and basil. Reduce heat and simmer for 10 minutes.

Serves 4

WOK-SEARED SOCKEYE SALMON

& VEGETABLES WITH SWEET & SOUR SAUCE

INGREDIENTS

8 oz.	sockeye salmon, cut in strips	250 g
1 tsp.	grated fresh ginger	5 mL
1 Tbsp.	cornstarch or rice flour	15 mL
to taste	salt and pepper	to taste
2 Tbsp.	vegetable oil	30 mL
1 cup	broccoli, cut in florets	250 mL
1	small carrot, peeled and thinly sliced	1
1	small onion, chopped	1
2	garlic cloves, thinly sliced	2
1 cup	tomato juice	250 mL
1 Tbsp.	rice vinegar	15 mL
1 Tbsp.	honey	15 mL
1 tsp.	sesame oil	5 mL
1	large tomato, cut in wedges	1

METHOD

In a small bowl, combine the salmon and grated ginger. Add the cornstarch or rice flour and season well with salt and pepper. Stir well to mix. Immediately heat a wok or skillet over medium-high heat. Add the oil and heat until almost smoking. Add the salmon and quickly stir-fry to coat with oil. Cook, stirring occasionally, until the salmon begins to brown and firms up (about 2 to 3 minutes). Transfer to a side plate and keep warm until needed.

Add the broccoli, carrot, and onion to the skillet. Heat until warmed through and beginning to brown, about 2 to 3 minutes. Add the garlic, tomato juice, vinegar, honey, and sesame oil. Bring to a boil and add the tomato wedges and cooked salmon. Stir to heat through and slightly thicken the sauce, about 1 to 2 minutes.

Serve over steamed rice.

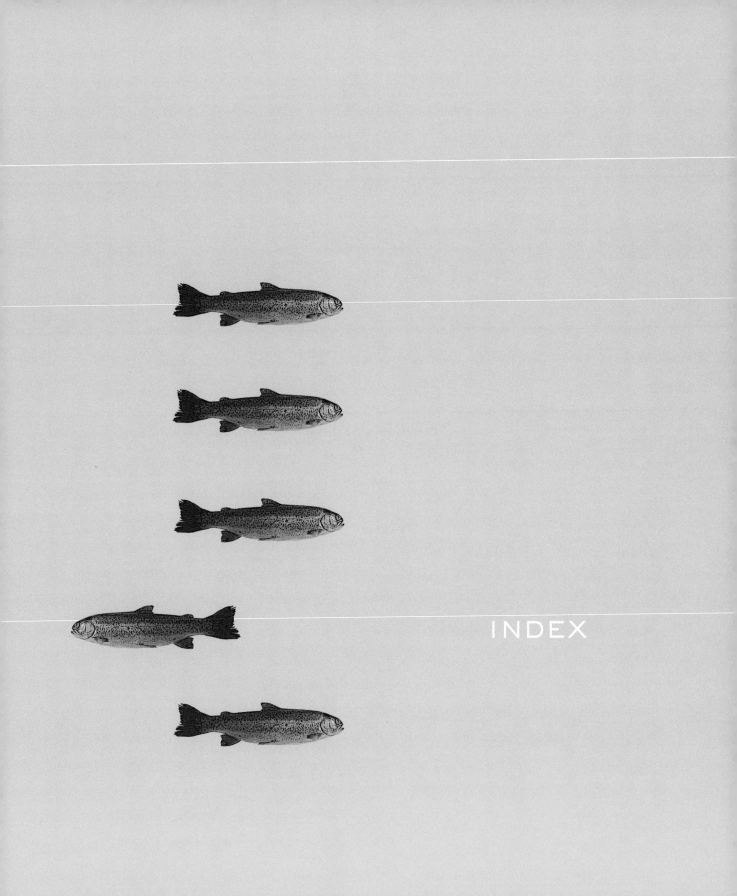

INDEX